GOOD ENOUGH

Jim,
I hope you enjoy!
Love & Light,

Carly Newberg

Live & light!
I hope you enjoy!

GOOD ENOUGH

BELIEVING BEAUTIFUL THROUGH TRAUMA, THROUGH LIFE, THROUGH DISORDER

CARLY NEWBERG

NEW DEGREE PRESS

COPYRIGHT © 2020 CARLY NEWBERG

GOOD ENOUGH
Believing Beautiful through Trauma, through Life, through Disorder

ISBN   978-1-63676-522-8   *Paperback*
            978-1-63676-057-5   *Kindle Ebook*
            978-1-63676-058-2   *Ebook*

To you, Kyle Gamez, for so graciously sharing your love and light with me and this world. Your spirit fueled the completion of this book and added a new dimension to the meaning of "good enough."

And to you, Papa, for showing me the beauty that comes from living a simple life and for always reminding me to look closer, think wiser, and love harder.

CONTENTS

———

"If we can't stand up to the never good enough and who do you think you are? we can't move forward."

—BRENÉ BROWN, THE GIFTS OF IMPERFECTION

INTRODUCTION

Do you ever find your mind so crowded with negativity all you want to do is run away in hopes you might be set free? When it becomes too loud to hear anything else, do you ever have the inclination—even just for a second—to put your head under a pillow and scream? If so, you're not alone. I refer to this noise as the monsters in my head.

My monsters are not new; they have been here for as long as I can remember. I would be on the bus home from kindergarten, completely overwhelmed and preoccupied with what sounded like a bunch of people talking over one another.

I couldn't tell you exactly what my monsters said to me then, but I can tell you how they made me feel. They made me feel heavy. They made me feel scared. They made me feel isolated. Each one had a different idea of what I needed to hear, and they all decided to talk at once and were more annoying than they were negative. I couldn't think clearly, and I couldn't escape them. It was exhausting.

Does anyone else hear this noise? I'd wonder.

As I started to mature, however, so did my monsters. Their voices became clearer, and they grew to be mean, bossy, and controlling.

You see, monsters aren't just thoughts. They are lies, false identities, untrue statements, and they are powerful.

When you're a kid, you're too fresh to fully understand and absorb these lies, false identities, and untrue statements. When you feel heavy, you go play or fall asleep on the couch. When you feel scared, you run to your parents and they tell you, *"It's okay, I'm right here."* When you feel isolated, you make a new friend without fear of rejection or judgment.

Over time, however, the world leaves a deeper imprint on us, and what our monsters have been trying to convince us of all along starts to sound a whole lot like the truth. Because not all thoughts are negative, especially when you're a child. But through circumstance and experience, the noise we *all* have in our heads can transform into something dark and ugly.

If we never learn how to see our monsters for what they are and develop new and healthy ways of thinking, we get caught looking at the world through a film of dust while thinking, *That's just the way it is. And if that's just the way it is, this must just be who I am.*

If I don't lose enough weight by the wedding, the day will be ruined.
I can't show my true self to the world, or I'll be rejected.
People can't be trusted; everyone leaves in the end.
My friends only like me because I'm pretty.

I am what I do.
I'm alone.

Evil thoughts not only invade our minds; they invade our bodies, our actions, and our words. They impact the way we treat ourselves and others, and they control the narratives we speak into the world and choose to live by. Those narratives become so ingrained in our second nature, we forget they're even lies.

Right now, there are too many men and women in the world struggling to see themselves as beautiful because of the power their monsters have over them. And I don't just mean beautiful in a physical sense, although that is important, too. When I say beautiful, what I really mean is knowing you are worthy, loved, and cared for.

As I revise this introduction now, I'm grieving the loss of my close friend, Kyle, who couldn't escape his monsters and made the decision to end his life. Although we'll never understand the exact reason why, I believe it had something to do with not feeling worthy, loved, and cared for.

I know of one group of people who have especially loud monsters: those suffering from eating disorders.

Did you know out of all mental illnesses, eating disorders have the second-highest mortality rate?[1] In the United States

---

1   Edward Chesney et al.,"Risks of All-Cause and Suicide Mortality in Mental Disorders: A Meta-Review," *World Psychiatry* 13, no. 2 (2014): 153-160.

alone, at least thirty million people are suffering from an eating disorder. That includes people of all ages and genders.[2,3]

Now, there are a variety of different reasons for this: genetic links, trauma, expectations set by others, family dynamics, media, fad diets. But the bottom line is, there are too many people clothed in lies from their monsters telling them who they are and who they must be to earn acceptance. People afraid of truth because welcoming the truth would mean saying goodbye to an identity they've clung to for years.

Maybe that's you, or maybe it used to be you.

Truth be told, it used to be me.

I spent years of my life living under the lie I wasn't ever enough, feeling like I had to prove myself and live up to lofty expectations my monsters set in front of me. I lost friends, time, and memories, covered in shame and paralyzed by both depression and anxiety.

This led to unhealthy coping strategies like suppressing emotions, running away from my problems (literally and metaphorically), starving myself, and stuffing myself.

2   Hudson I. James et al.,"The Prevalence and Correlates of Eating Disorders
    in the National Comorbidity Survey Replication," *Biological Psychiatry*,
    61, no. 3 (2007): 348–358.

3   Daniel Le Grange et al., "Eating Disorder Not Otherwise Specified Pre-
    sentation in the Us Population," *International Journal of Eating Disorders*,
    45, no. 5 (2012): 711-718.

Under the umbrella of eating disorders, I fell somewhere in between anorexia nervosa, bulimia, and exercise addiction. After close to six years and through my healing journey, I've come to find I'm not the only one who struggles to know and believe their worth.

Because it doesn't matter how many times someone looks you in the eyes and tells you you're beautiful, you have to believe it—and if you don't—you have to keep fighting.

I wrote this book because I used to feel alone in my fighting, and now I know I'm not alone when it comes to battling thoughts of unworthiness, fear, guilt, and shame. I wrote this book because I believe we don't have to succumb to darkness forever. Even in the darkest of pits, there lies restoration.

Many of my eating disorder behaviors evolved from unaddressed trauma. My parents divorced when I was young, and the consequences of their separation left a painful wound I didn't start to process until much later in life.

One of the behaviors I possessed during my disorder was purging—that is, getting rid of the food I ate after a meal. I did this by taking laxatives and excessively exercising. It turns out, this is not uncommon for those struggling to process trauma.

> Binge eating and/or purging appear to be behaviors that facilitate reducing the hyperarousal or anxiety associated with trauma, and the numbing, avoidance, and even forgetting of traumatic experiences. These behaviors are reinforcing, making it difficult to break

the cycle. As a result, traumatic experiences and their destructive effects are not effectively processed and continue to cause problems.[4]

My illness was an attempt to protect my internal self by perfecting my external self. I was impacted by a false portrayal of beauty, weight stigma, fad diets, and unqualified individuals offering up health advice, but only because I was dealing with something deeper and thought being skinny would make it go away.

Only, it didn't. Instead, I felt locked inside a prison. As I got smaller, my monsters got louder and demanded even more from me. And guess what? At the end of each day, my wound was still there, behind the makeup, behind the running, and behind the mask.

What I've come to realize is unprocessed trauma is the culprit of unfinished healing. We all have to go through and work through the hard stuff to appreciate the good stuff—that's part of life.

Yet, completing this task without guidance or company is grueling, which is why I believe with my whole heart the best way we can learn is through the stories of others... and man, do I have stories.

This book wasn't easy for me to write, and getting all of this down on paper is the most vulnerable thing I've ever done,

---

4   Timothy D. Brewerton et al., "Eating Disorders, Trauma, and Comorbidity: Focus on PTSD," *Eating Disorders: The Journal of Treatment & Prevention*, 15, no. 4 (2007): 285-304.

yet I knew I wouldn't be able to rest until it was finished. God's been telling me from the beginning this is a book the world needs.

This is a book I needed when I was unwell, and it's a book people like my friend, Kyle, need.

What you're about to read is my story of transformation— how I went from being an anxious presence in just about every situation life threw at me, to being someone who isn't controlled by her monsters and is able to find joy, identity, and belonging independent of my circumstances.

I share moments when I've chosen to believe false narratives through raw and transparent journal entries. Over time, I've had to rewrite these narratives while learning to trust in a God more steady and secure than my present-day troubles.

There've been many times when I've felt the world is against me. Times when I've doubted God's presence and have wondered, *Does He even care?*

During one of these periods, I was reminded the adversity I face in this life is only *branches beneath our feet.* Not *my* feet, but *our* feet.

What does that mean exactly? It means you can walk through and overcome anything you face (both big and small) and you don't have to do it alone.

At first, recovering from my eating disorder felt impossible, and I'll be honest, it's been a long journey. I'd wake up and wonder what life would be like if I wasn't so consumed by my image. *Will there ever be a day I don't obsess over everything I eat and feel shame afterward?*

The answer is, yes.

You could be in a forest of unknowns and still walk out the other end because Jesus would be there with you, the most relational human being to ever walk this Earth. With Him by your side, your problems don't stand a chance.

And if you don't believe that now, that's okay. You will by the end of these pages because both He and I give you full permission to take up space just as you are.

So, if you're ready to walk out the other side of the forest, this book is for you. It's time to embrace the sunshine, feel the warmth on your face, and the love all around you.

The messages in this book are specifically tailored to those struggling with an eating disorder or disordered patterns around food and body (past or present). However, I've written it in a way that will resonate with many. If you've dealt with trauma of any kind or the haunting feeling of never being enough, you will find both strength and comfort in these pages.

More than anything, I want to offer you a new perspective, free from the film of dust I mentioned earlier—insight that has helped me and will help you too. I pray this book is not only a resource but a friend most of all.

On the other hand, if the topics I've covered thus far are completely foreign to you, I want to educate you because I promise there is someone in your life who has or still is battling their monsters, and you need to read this book for them.

So come with me. Don't put this book down and rule it out as "not for you" because I can guarantee you will leave with, if nothing else, the empathy required and the tools necessary to walk alongside those struggling when they need it most.

My monsters, no matter how dark and ugly, need to be shared because there is strength in numbers.

I'm in process, and I'm starting to see that is a beautiful thing. I hope you view your process as beautiful too, and you will allow me to take part in your journey with you. Together, I believe we will grow and flourish into greater versions of ourselves as we start to grasp the powerful truth that we are good enough.

PART 1

FAMILY AND RELATIONSHIPS

CHAPTER 1

WHISPERS, SECRETS, AND SURPRISES

———

"So often, I have felt troubled and guilty bearing witness to my pain... Somehow telling the truth as I know it makes me feel like a bad person—as if I'm making my pain up, as if I'm hurting others by saying things about them. But the unshake-able bottom of all of this is that I'm not making things up. If I have unkind things to say, it's because I've experienced unkind things. And so, my only guide in this witnessing is to be accurate and honest. While I am not a victim, I didn't ask for certain shaping experiences to happen to me... In truth, if I had experienced different things, I would have different things to say."

— MARK NEPO[5]

———

5   Mark Nepo, *The Book of Awakening: Having the Life You Want by Being Present to the Life You Have* (Newburyport: Conari Press, 2000), 63.

When I was a child, I did everything I could to appear blameless in front of my parents. I wanted to be "good" and do things "right" because I feared what would happen if I didn't.

Things that should have been fun as a kid were stressful. I'd be painting at the table with my mom and would break down crying because my flower didn't look as good as hers did. Never mind the fact she was years ahead of me in the painting department.

I felt similar with the kids at school, and this behavior carried on through my teenage and adult years in the form of an eating disorder. However, to tell that story, I first have to give some background to the events prior.

The thing is, eating disorders are not as one-dimensional as people think they are. It's not as simple as wanting to be skinny, which is a common assumption. Instead, it is a multidimensional puzzle that for most (including me) dates back to when they were young.

It's important to note an eating disorder is a mental illness, not something a person chooses. In addition, it's not wise to assume every person with an eating disorder is emaciated. In fact, a majority of those suffering aren't underweight, but more on that later.[6]

What I want you to know for now is my eating disorder was not anyone's fault—especially not my parents. As you read

6   "Eating Disorder Myths," National Eating Disorders Association, accessed September 3, 2020.

the remainder of this chapter and the ones to follow, you might be tempted to think it is. Yet as I said before, eating disorders are multidimensional and include *many* layers.

My parents are human, and they did their best. The reality that some of their actions negatively impacted me isn't congruent with the idea that if only they were more, I'd be different.

That's not what this book is about. Rather, this book is about finding enough in the not enough, which includes my mom and dad.

The Moment Everything Changed

When I was eight years old, my parents got into the first big fight I had ever witnessed them having, and things went from being normal to drastically different for everyone in the family—that is, me, my mom, my dad, and my brother, who is five years older than me.

It all started when I got home from school one afternoon and heard the two of them yelling at the top of their lungs. Worried, I ran into the house and headed straight to the kitchen where the noise was coming from and, within seconds, spotted my brother through the sliding glass door jumping over the fence in our backyard.

This led to even more of an uproar between my parents, and when they turned around and saw me, my mom came over and tried to calm the puzzled look on my face.

"Honey, I want you to go and grab your baby doll, okay? We're going on a little drive to look for your brother, and then we're going to stay at Grandma's for a couple of days, okay? Can you do that for me?"

After grabbing my baby doll from my room, I came back out to the living room and realized both of my parents were no longer in the house. I could hear more yelling in the distance and made my way out to the driveway.

"Carly, stay right there. You're not going anywhere," my dad told me.

Growing up, my dad was stern and quick to put me and my brother in our place when we didn't listen. I feared doing things "wrong" more with him than my mom because I couldn't handle the condemnation that followed. I was sensitive and shut down at the sound of loud voices or correction.

In his book *Personality Types*, Don Richard Riso explains this fear when talking about Enneagram Ones, which is my personality type:

> These children learned to fear condemnation and to avoid it by always attempting to be blameless. The principal message from their father was, "You are not acceptable as you are, you must be better, always better." Their own wishes and feelings were rarely if ever countenanced; instead, these children always had to toe the line to avoid being criticized or condemned...

Ones were not allowed to be children but were forced to become little adults before their time.[7]

What I needed in a moment like this was compassion and gentleness, which I received from my mom. At the same time, I didn't want to upset my dad.

"Don't listen to your dad, Carly. Get in the truck for Mommy, please."

It was a tug of war between the two of them and I was in the middle, confused and scared.

My mom was already in the driver's seat, and my dad was standing by the driver's door. He kept repeating himself, one of his trademarks.

"You're not taking the truck. Get out now before I call the cops," he demanded.

Cops?

Before I could say a word, the shrieking sound of my mom's voice and her torn skirt echoed throughout the neighborhood. The yelling escalated again, and I stood in the driveway crying louder, begging them to *please stop.* I closed my eyes and gripped my baby doll as hard as I could.

---

7   Don Richard Riso, *Personality Types: Using the Enneagram for Self-Discovery* (Boston: Houghton Mifflin, 1987), 279.

An eternity later, one of our neighbors came out and silenced both of my parents, telling them if they didn't stop, *he* was going to call the cops. He patted my back, told me it was going to be okay, and then told both of my parents to look at how much they were scaring me.

The rest of that afternoon was full of runny noses and a truck ride up and down the streets in the small town of Lebanon, Oregon where I grew up. Once we found my brother, I blamed him for the fight that broke out between our parents. Of course, it was his fault.

Mommy and Daddy never fight, and if he would just follow the rules and do what he is told, none of this would have happened.

When we pulled into the driveway to our grandparents' house, I realized there may have been more to the story. "Why aren't we going home?" I asked my mom.

"We're just going to stay a couple of days at Grandma's, okay, sweetie? I promise nothing is wrong, and we will be back home soon."

I believed my mom in this moment. *Surely, it was just miscommunication. They will work it out. The trusted adults in my life are right, I don't have anything to worry about. We'll go back home, and things will be okay. Daddy will go back to paying the bills, and Mommy will go back to tucking me in before bed. They are a team.*

But my mom only kept part of her promise. We did eventually make it back to the house on Filbert Street. Was it home?

No. Was everything okay? Nowhere near. My dad had taken his stuff and moved out, and there were lots of tears and questions my mom didn't know how to answer. I went from being completely blind to what was becoming of their almost fourteen years of marriage to being completely submerged into the thick of their problems without answers.

At times, it felt like even the teachers and staff at school knew more about my mom and dad's situation than I did. They would look at me with wide eyes and whispers, asking me how I was. My friends' parents would ask if I was okay, and I never knew how to reply because it was clear they knew something I didn't.

Kids at school tried to help me see the silver lining in divorce. I would have two rooms, two birthdays, double the Christmas presents, everything an eight-year-old could ever ask for. Besides, I still got to see my dad every other weekend, and my mom eventually worked up the strength to battle against her emotions and be present for my brother and me.

Then things seemed to look up. One of my close friends in grade school invited me to go to summer camp with her at Big Lake, right outside of Sisters, Oregon in the Willamette National Forest.

Her parents did both my parents and me a huge favor, which I will forever be grateful for. My mom and dad were able to figure out the details of their divorce while I went kayaking, swimming, and exploring in a forest where there was no place for fear.

Before I left, my mom hugged me extra tight and told me she would see me in a week. I kissed her goodbye and acknowledged what she said, when really all I could focus on was the thought of going to my first summer camp ever with one of my friends. I was preoccupied, excited, and eager. Little did I know, my mom's words would ring in my ears for months afterward.

Memories on Replay

Big Lake Camp is where I heard God's name and joined hands with a group of young people to pray before dinner for the first time.

While away, I had almost forgotten about everything going on at home. What I experienced was magical. Sitting in a circle laughing with the other young girls in my cabin at night, sleeping in bunk beds, and waking up each day to bathe in the lake at sunrise before a day full of games and snacks.

It wasn't until the last day of camp that I was unpleasantly reminded of the catastrophe at home.

I walked beside my friend, thinking about how lucky I was to have her. I thought about how God must be a really cool guy since they had an entire camp designed around just Him, and I wondered what being a Christian even meant. I knew if it was anything like the last week had been, I wanted to sign up.

I discovered later on in my relationship with Jesus that a relationship with Him is so much more than a simple application process.

When I walked outside of the gift shop, everyone's parents were there to pick them up. My friend was telling her mom and dad how great camp had been while I scanned the audience of people, looking for my mom. Seconds later, I spotted my dad. Tall, slender, with dark and curly hair, and boots—not my mom.

When I asked my dad where my mom was, he said she had stuff to do and he came to get me instead. When I reminded him she promised she would be there to get me, he said we would talk about it in the car. This is when I knew things were not alright.

Out of all the memories I made at camp that have faded over the years, this is the one moment I haven't been able to forget. Over and over, it plays in my head, and with each passing year, my heart cries more and more for the young girl who had no idea her world was about to change in ways she couldn't ever imagine.

When we got in the car, my dad tried to avoid talking about why he was there instead of my mom by asking me a million questions about how camp was. I answered him thoughtfully, and between each question, I urged him to fill me in on what was happening.

I don't remember the exact words he used, but eventually, my dad did tell me the truth—or rather, part of the truth. And as a child, knowing only part of the truth is almost worse than not knowing anything at all. After he spoke, I wished I could have wiped my memory clean to stay a kid for just a little while longer.

Not only were my parents getting a divorce, but my dad was granted full custody of both my brother and me. We would be staying with him at his parents' home for a short time. We'd still see our mom on the weekends, he promised. Nothing was going to change. It was just temporary, he said.

However, just like the voice of my mom telling me she promised to pick me up from camp, my dad's words remained at the forefront of my mind, playing over and over for many months.

Broken Promises

After the first week of living at my grandparents' house with my dad and brother, I began asking when I would see my mom next. He quickly assured me the next weekend we would see her. They couldn't make it work that weekend. When another week had gone by, I couldn't wait. I arrived home from school, and my dad shrugged me off. He told me something had come up and that weekend wasn't going to work anymore, either.

I missed my mom. It had never been more than a weekend where I didn't see her. As a young child with very little patience, I continued to ask when I would see my mother.

"He is lying to you, Carly," my brother would say. "It's been six months... We're not going to see her. He's lying."

My brother and I loved to push each other's buttons. It seemed like every day we would get into some kind of argument or teasing match. And I wanted to think him telling me we wouldn't be seeing my mom was him just trying to rile me up, yet deep down I knew he was telling the truth. Out of everyone else, he was giving me the naked and raw reality, even though it hurt.

All I could think about was the promise my dad had made. He promised. He looked down into my innocent eyes—into eyes never exposed to evil and full of curiosity—and he promised. If I had learned anything in the eight years of my life, it was promises were never to be broken, especially not by your parents.

At the time, it felt like everyone I thought I could trust had completely turned their backs on me. Even my friends at school started to act weird when they were with me. They looked at me differently, they talked to me differently, and some didn't talk to me at all. I understand now politics within an elementary school are no joke. For some moms, gossip is their full-time job.

To have my mom go from being a part of the PTA, designing all the props and scenes for school plays, chaperoning field trips, and leaving me cute notes every day in my lunch pail, to not being present at all, created quite a bit of gossip. It also created repetitive stress that I now know as trauma.

Trauma is the result of one or many incidents an individual finds either emotionally disturbing or life-threatening. In the long run, these incidents affect the functioning of the individual's well-being on a mental, physical, social, emotional, and/or spiritual level. Trauma can happen at any age, but with children especially, it leaves long-term effects on their developing brains.[8]

What I experienced as a young girl was certainly traumatic, given I'm still working through the hurtful memories I carry. The long-term effects of trauma on children have been termed as Adverse Childhood Experiences (ACEs), and in the United States alone, 62 percent of adults have had at least one ACE.[9]

It's easy to look at someone who is binge eating and assume they have no self-control. "Just don't grab seconds. I mean *seriously*, how hard is it to stop eating when you are full?" What's more difficult, is to look beneath the surface to understand the so-called "problem" is only a symptom of something deeper.

I've felt judged by myself and others for the choices I've made, and I've judged others for the choices they've made. But through educating myself, I've started to understand how it's not me or other people to blame. There is always a trigger that onsets and leads us to behave the way we do, and for a vast majority, trauma is the trigger.

> People affected by trauma may develop coping mechanisms to help alleviate the emotional and/or physical pain they feel as a result of trauma. Sometimes these strategies involve maladaptive behaviors such as unhealthy eating, tobacco use, or drug and alcohol use. These coping mechanisms may provide some

8   "What Is Trauma?" Trauma-Informed Care Implementation Resource Center, accessed August 22, 2020.

9   Ibid.

relief, but they can also simultaneously contribute to anxiety, social isolation, and chronic diseases.[10]

So, ask yourself, *In my story, what unhealthy behaviors have I used to put a blanket over what was hurting me?*

My Story, My Perspective

To this day, I don't know all the details of the custodial battle between my parents because both of them will tell you a different story.

If you ask my dad why he was granted full custody, he will say he took my brother and me out of unsafe conditions when my mom was on drugs and unable to be a parent. This is why he had to get a restraining order on her and why we weren't allowed to see her.

If you ask my mom why my dad was granted full custody, she will tell you it was my dad's way of hurting her. He cheated on my mom, was caught in the scheme of things, and didn't like it. My dad had money, which granted him more power and authority in the courtroom, and it wasn't until we were taken away from her that she started dabbling in drugs.

With both of these explanations, the only story I know to be true is my own, and that's the story I'm here to tell—my experience and my perspective.

---

10   Ibid.

Why? Because for too long I stood quiet while everyone around me got to tell *their* story. The truth is, I needed a book like this when *I* was struggling, and I want to use my words to comfort you if *you're* struggling.

The divorce of my parents made me feel alone and judged. It put a pause on my childhood for years, and even though I felt like a black sheep, I tried to control my feelings by suppressing them. I'd cover up with a mask until my childlike self would burst out of the shell begging for attention.

In *The Book of Awakening*, Mark Nepo expresses the phenomenon of hiding perfectly:

From the agonies of Kindergarten, when we were first teased or made fun of in the midst of all our innocence, we have all struggled in one way or another with hiding what is obvious about us. No one plans this. It is not a conspiracy, but rather an inevitable and hurtful passage from knowing only ourselves to knowing the world. The problem is that many of us never talk about it, or even get told that our 'green hair' is beautiful, or that we don't need to hide, no matter what anyone says on the way to lunch. And so, we often conclude that to know the world we must hide ourselves. Nothing could be farther from the truth. It is an ancient, unspoken fact of being that blackmail is only possible if we believe that we have something to hide. The inner corollary of this is that worthless feelings arise when we believe, however briefly, that who we are is not enough.[11]

---

11 Nepo, *The Book of Awakening*, 6.

In the next three chapters, I'm going to give some context for my relationships with my mom, my dad, and my brother because they will provide more depth on where I've been and what I've come out of. In other words, I will show how the onset of my parents' divorce had a domino effect on just about every area of my life: how I view friendships, how I view love, how I view God, and most of all, how I view myself.

These are the layers all holding the unique encounters and events that shaped who I've become and who I'm still becoming.

I want you to walk away with knowledge of pivotal moments in *your* life and how they've impacted your perspective. Are you stuck hiding? If so, I want you to walk away with faith—faith that whatever you're experiencing (whether that be negative body image, worthlessness, or hopelessness), none of it is too big for God to handle.

Going back through our past can be useful for identifying triggers to certain behaviors, unhealthy coping devices, and why those devices have helped us cope in the first place. It can also serve as a tool, giving us ideas to successfully manage our triggers and choose new coping mechanisms to help and not harm us.

The last thing I will say is, if you've fallen victim to divorce and all that is to follow, I hope you've been able to find some sense of freedom and relief. Regardless of how smooth or rough the divorce was, it's a hard thing to go through. However, with a new lens, I've found the pain and confusion becomes a little easier to bear and with time, will not be as heavy of a memory to carry with you.

So, join me as I share with you the broken lens I once saw through, and the beautiful one I've come to know and trust. You may find there is a new lens for you to look through in your own life too.

CHAPTER 2

MISSING MOM

———

I love that in order to receive God's gifts, I don't have to wait my whole life. When I give my trust over to Him now, I can walk in constant Light that overcomes darkness.

Before the divorce, I watched my mom cook dinner every night while my dad would come home from a long day of work and sit on the couch with a beer in front of the TV. We never ate around the table as a family, and dinner time as a kid is not a pleasant memory.

I never remember my mom eating dinner. Come to think of it, I don't even remember her sitting down while we ate. I think she was too irritated with my dad by the time she finished cooking, or she just snuck bites as she cooked so there was time to clean up the kitchen and help my brother and me with homework and our bedtime routine before school the next day.

My mother ran a daycare business in our home and watched close to fifteen kids every day. She was always making sure we had what we needed, even when she was exhausted. Waking us up in the morning with mellow, feel-good music on the stereo, she'd help me pick out my outfit, make breakfast, and do my hair as I knelt with my nose lightly brushing against the edge of the kitchen counter.

I still remember the smell of that kitchen counter. Not just the counter, but everything in our home had a scent of love and a warmth that radiated from within my mom.

Before things went south with my parents, losing her was never on my list of worries. She didn't just care for me in the ways I needed, she listened to me and loved me with a fierce kind of love I still have yet to comprehend. Her kids were always her top priority, and she was quick to meet our needs before her own. She did make sure we had the clothes, food, and shelter we needed but also ensured we had the support, affection, and instruction we needed.

Yearning for Someone to Listen

When I started to understand the reality of my parents' divorce and what it meant for my life, the world no longer appeared as colorful as it did before. I was a cheerful, happy kid, yet struggled to find anything wholesome and good in a world where I was surrounded by what felt like lies and deceit. Things were not okay, yet people around me continued to act like they were.

My mom has told me over and over she never in a million years thought my dad would try to get full custody of my brother and me. She worried about the house being taken away, not having a car, deciding who would get what furniture, but never did she think she had to worry about her kids being taken from her.

If my dad wanted to be a full-time parent, he sure didn't act like it. Much of the responsibility that came with having two kids fell on my mom, not him.

Looking back, it's not hard to see why he was granted full custody. He was the breadwinner in our family, and it put my mom at a major disadvantage. My dad had the funds to hire one of the best lawyers around and to get the help he needed. Sure, she ran her daycare, but it didn't provide near the same amount of money or benefits he earned as a salesman of an ice cream company he'd been with for almost twenty-five years.

My mom's daycare business ended at the same time the divorce took place, and then she was left unemployed. As the courts saw it, my dad was "stable," and she wasn't. Yet, I never felt without anything when I was with my mom. Rather, I felt abundantly taken care of and my needs were met before I even knew there was a need.

A couple of years after the divorce, my mom got pregnant back to back with my younger sister and brother, whom I will introduce later. While living in a tiny apartment with my siblings, she built me a loft above their bed so I had my own space when I came to stay.

She's one of the most resourceful people I know and somehow always managed. She knew the schedule of churches handing out food boxes every month and could make a feast using a few random ingredients.

If money was tight or if any of us kids ever needed anything, she'd look around and see what she could sell. I've never met anyone with such eBay-savvy skills as my mother. I knew every time we passed a garage sale, free sign, or thrift store, there was no escape route; we had to stop. She'd find something priced for six dollars, worth six hundred dollars. It was insane. My mom isn't only resourceful, but everything she does, she does with love.

That is the difference between my mom and dad. I used to tell her I didn't care if we were living in a cardboard box on the side of the road, I'd still choose her.

If you were to compare my parents' professional resumes, my mom's resume would come up short. There's not usually a box on custody paperwork where writing "homemaker" or "eBay expert" is acceptable. There's not a section to explain the quality time and moments you've had with your kids.

Instead, they want to know how much money you make and whether you can provide basic necessities for your kids. I get these things are important, but in cases like mine, I just wish someone had stopped looking at the paperwork and looked at me.

For nearly two years following the last day of Big Lake Camp, I rarely saw my mom. She had a new boyfriend, who is now my younger siblings' dad, and they moved to Grants

Pass, Oregon when contact with my brother and I was cut off completely.

She would attempt to come visit from time to time, but the chances of her seeing me were slim. I had a birthday party not long after my mom left and asked my dad if she could be there. He agreed, yet when it came time to celebrate my birthday, she was nowhere to be found.

I was confused until my dad ended up telling me she couldn't make it. Devastated, I later came to find out the reason she couldn't make it was because he told her she wasn't allowed there.

Once, my school was preparing to go on a field trip to a waterpark, and I didn't have a swimsuit. I told my dad I needed one, and he told me we'd make it work.

Make it work? I wondered. *With what?* There was already enough talk going on at school, and I didn't want to add not having a proper swimsuit to the mix.

During one of the short conversations my mom and I had over the phone, I was able to stress to her I had a field trip coming up next week and my dad wouldn't get me a swimsuit. She told me not to worry, she would make sure I had one. The following week, I was watching TV when I noticed a car pull up in the driveway; it was my mom. I sprinted out of the door to where she was.

Latching on tightly with my arms around her waist, I worried what would happen if I were to let go. But before we even had a chance to say anything, my dad's girlfriend at the time (who not long before was my mom's best friend) pulled me away and demanded my mom leave or the police would have her arrested.

I didn't get it. All she was doing was dropping off a swimsuit for me because she knew how important it was. She understood me. She was my mother. The parent who knew how to be a parent. But in my dad's eyes, she didn't know how to be a parent since she—in his words—had become dependent on drugs.

Regardless, not being allowed contact with her made for two of the hardest years of my life. My dad kept all the letters and cards that were sent, disregarded any phone calls or gifts, and informed school officials he had a restraining order on my mom, and she was not to see me. I found out later, my dad never had a restraining order on her. She was the one who had a restraining order on him.

I longed for someone to talk to when my mom was no longer around, and one day remembered one of the last things she said to me before our separation. She said to write down everything and to keep a journal because she didn't want to miss anything. So, I started writing to her almost every day.

June 6, 2006
Dear Mommy,
I miss you. I'm crying right now. I wish I could sleep with you. I can't go to sleep without thinking of you. I love you so much and I want to see you really bad mommy. I miss doing every-thing with you. I always listen to number one on the Curious

George CD you got me when I write to you. I love you and am
very tired. I'll try to stop crying, but I can't.
Love, Carly Shane

Not only was I cut off from my mom after the divorce, but I was seldom allowed to see anyone on her side of the family because of my dad's fear of losing control.

My mom's family is very large, and to make sure I wasn't talking to any of them was not an easy task. However, it was something he thought necessary at the time and succeeded at doing.

There were a couple of family members from my mom's side my dad did trust, but it still took a lot of contemplation before he'd agree to let me stay with them. He'd have to talk to them first and hear some sort of affirmation to let him know he was doing the right thing by taking my brother and me away from our mother.

For instance, if I was going to stay with my aunt Leanna, who I was the closest with, she'd have to agree to a certain extent my mom was in the wrong and my dad was in the right.

I don't know if my aunt truly felt this way. Still, I am thankful regardless of her opinion she had compassion for the situation and understood the need for an eight-year-old girl to know her mom.

A few times, my aunt Leanna let me call my mom and talk to her for as long as I wished, and there were even a couple of occasions where we stayed the night together at my aunt's and didn't tell my dad. If it weren't for those moments, I don't know if I would have made it through those two years.

What loosened my father's grip of control and eased him into the idea of us seeing our mother again was finding out she was pregnant. I'll never forget the day he came into my room to tell me we were going to meet my mom down at the park.

I almost didn't believe him and got a sudden pit of nervousness in my stomach. It had been so long since I last saw her, and I couldn't help but wonder why my dad had suddenly changed his mind. When I asked him, he said she had something important to tell us.

We arrived at the park that day and my mom, brother, and I embraced amidst the grass, letting out tears of joy and relief to be with each other once again. We then sat down at a picnic table nearby, my brother and I both eager to hear her news.

Within only a few minutes, she was pushing across the table two sticky note memo pads with a pregnancy center logo at the bottom. It took a second for me to realize this was her way of telling us she was pregnant with my little sister, but once it clicked, I started to see color once again.

I asked my mom over and over, before the divorce, if she could please have another baby. I wanted so badly to have a sister, and each time she laughed and said, "Sorry, sweetie, that's not going to happen. Mommy's done having babies."

We came to find out later Marley Jane (named to match my name, Carly Shane) was a surprise, and my brother Linkin

Ray, who entered our lives thirteen months after Marley, was another surprise. My mom calls them her "surprise, surprise!"

We all agree Marley and Linkin have been two of the best gifts to ever be given, but Marley's arrival especially changed all of our lives for the better. I think it's no coincidence I spent so long asking for a sister, and she was born on my brother's birthday. As cliche as it sounds, she was our saving grace.

During my mom's pregnancy with Marley, she moved back to the Lebanon area to be closer to me, my brother, and our family, and my dad started allowing us to have four-hour, supervised visitations with her. Those four hours certainly weren't long enough, but we cherished every moment.

Stuck in the Past

Four-hour visitations with my mom eventually turned into unsupervised overnight visits, which then turned into weekend-long visits. Because of my sister (and my brother's approaching arrival), my dad was confident she was no longer using drugs and thought it acceptable to let us continue seeing her.

As I got older, I often pushed the limits he had set and would try to stay with my mom for longer periods. The answer was always "no," but I still thought it was worth a try.

"Why?" I'd ask.
"Because I said so."
Classic.

He and I continued to grow apart as I got older, and my mom and I became closer. He despised the fact she and I were building a relationship, and if I would spend more than two nights at her house, he'd demand I come home.

Only, I didn't have to ask my dad why he was demanding me to come home. I already knew the reason: he craved control.

He knew a big part of the bonding my mom and I experienced was caused by the abuse we both felt from him. He knew what happened was not right, regardless of the state my mom was in. He was insecure, and control over others made him feel better about himself. At least, that's how it seemed.

After my older brother moved out of our dad's, he lived with our mom for a while, and I was always complaining about how unfair it was. I wanted to live there, too. I hated leaving her house and wished I could see her whenever I wanted. She was my mom, for heaven's sake!

When I got my license, seeing her whenever I wanted became much easier. She moved into a bigger house with John, her new boyfriend at the time, who just so happened to be my friend Rosie's uncle and both of my parents' friend.

Don't ask me why my parents found it necessary to date each other's friends. I think it must be a small-town thing.

Seeing Rosie's uncle and my mom together was odd at first. However, I soon got used to their relationship and found myself over at their home often as a way to escape my dad.

My mom has always been one of the closest people to me and being without her presence (even for short amounts of time) felt crippling.

Almost immediately after turning eighteen, I moved into their home, eager to make up for lost time while also nervous to be living with my mom after nearly ten years of separation.

Once I settled in and the initial excitement had passed, my mom and I got hit with a whole new set of concerns. I often tell people we went through everything an eight-year-old girl and her mother go through, only it was when I was eighteen.

She'd try to parent me on things I'd already taught myself, and whenever that happened, we'd both be reminded of our time apart, her not getting to do her job as a parent, and me being forced to do a job I wasn't yet qualified for.

There were a lot of times my mom apologized for not being there, and there were a lot of times I made her feel guilty for not being there.

When Marley and Linkin would talk back to her or do something disrespectful, I'd burn with anger.

If only they knew how good they had it.
At least they have a mom.
When I was their age, I dreamt of my mom being there to tell me what to do.

She would be helping the kids with their homework or making them an after-school snack, and I'd get quiet or moody as I thought about how those things were taken away from me.

Every time she volunteered on a school field trip, hung a piece of the kids' artwork on the fridge, taught them how to garden, and tucked them in at night, it was like another log being tossed upon an already wobbly stack of built-up resentment.

And when the stack fell over, I'd act out, saying nothing was the matter when everything was the matter. I'd throw things and yell at Marley and Linkin like it was their fault when in reality they were the reason why my mom and I were allowed visitations in the first place.

I'd run or journal to keep my fits to myself and to avoid the mental clutter and emotional pain I was in. I didn't have a relationship with God like I do now; otherwise, I would have prayed and most likely lashed out at Him, too. But at the time, I felt like my issues were too messy even for Him. It's no wonder why after moving in with my mom, my eating disorder worsened, which you will see in later chapters.

The important thing to know is control over food and exercise is what made me feel safe. I had yet to learn how to control my monsters, and I carried a lot of resentment. Because I also never processed my past, trying to live in the present was a nightmare, especially because I was trying to do it alone.

It's embarrassing to admit, but the whole year I lived with my mom, I'd make her tuck me in at night when she tucked the kids in. I was a senior in high school, and I'd ask her to pack my lunch. I wanted her help with my homework even though I could have figured it out on my own. I needed her full attention, and if I didn't have it, I'd just pull the "You weren't there" card to remind her how bad I was still hurting.

When I think back to this time, I recognize how much I expected out of not just my mom, but my dad, too. Because I strived for perfection in my own life, I searched for it in the lives of those around me.

I mentioned the Enneagram earlier when I referred to myself as a One, the Perfectionist or Reformer. The Enneagram is a tool used for personal growth and discovery, and during my recovery I took a deeper look at resources on the Enneagram to try and understand myself better.

Out of all the books I've read, people I've talked to, and podcasts I've listened to, Don Richard Riso, who you will see me quote often, has been able to explain the tension a One faces better than anyone else when he states:

> Ironically, Ones vent their anger most unfairly at others when they are angry primarily with themselves for not being perfect. Instead of resolving their own disordered feelings, average to unhealthy Ones find fault everywhere else. Their self-righteous anger makes Ones aggressive; however, the one is not an aggressive personality type as such. Actually, Ones are compliant to their ideals, since the ideal is a yardstick by which they measure everything, including themselves. The aggression in their personalities is

an expression of anger at themselves and others for not complying perfectly to the ideal.[12]

We all want our parents to meet the ideal, and comparison doesn't help us in accepting them when they don't. The thing is, my mom wasn't the gem I made her out to be as a child, and when she didn't meet the ideal as I got older, I bullied her into trying harder instead of working on myself.

She didn't listen to me as much as I wished she would.
She interrupted me and took my moments of vulnerability and made them about her.
She never answered when I called and needed her most.
She was always late.

I still notice my mom's faults and failures today, and I'd be lying if I said it doesn't sting, knowing my brother and sister get her for *all* of their childhood.

As I write this during the COVID-19 pandemic, I think of earlier in the week when she sent me a photo of her and my brother having what she referred to as a "bonding moment." It was a group message and at the very end there was a text that said, *"miss you all so much."*

I called the following day after telling myself I wouldn't. I wanted her to call *me* for once to check in and see how *I* was. Although she had posted on Facebook multiple times that day, she didn't answer. That hurt because I had just moved to a new city where I didn't know anyone and wasn't working.

---

12   Riso, *Personality Types,* 280.

I was spending almost every day alone in quarantine, and my mental state was declining.

It started to become about me again, about how *I* feel and what *I* need. But the truth is, my mom has come a long way and is trying harder to be there for me every day, especially in a year as trying as 2020. She has shown up for me over and over, that I know. I also know there are moments when my siblings have been envious of me, the bond *we* share, and they also need her.

So, do my mom's actions still affect me? Yes, absolutely. But do I angrily force her to do better? No.

The difference is I now see my mom and me as equals, and my yardstick of judgment doesn't get to determine the worth of either of us. The expectation isn't perfection anymore. The same is true of my dad, as you will see in the next chapter.

The biggest shift to come from this all is my hope isn't in myself or the people around me like it used to be. My hope is in Jesus.

I know now whatever emotion I am feeling, He can handle it. In fact, He wants to help me carry and process my emotions. They don't scare Him. They don't make Him uncomfortable. He doesn't turn a blind eye and tell me I'm too much.

God gave us all emotions, and He's not expecting us to follow after the toxic trend of hyper-positivity. Know it's okay to be sad, angry, numb, and hopeless. It's okay to not have answers or quick fixes to your problems. It's okay to not be able to find joy in difficult situations right away, or to find the "reason" for something because everyone around you keeps saying *everything happens for a reason.*

This truth has set me free in a lot of ways, and I think if I would have understood this when I was younger, I would have coped differently. But being a perfectionist, I thought I was so clever in trying to handle things on my own and hide from God. It's a good thing He always finds us and picks up the pieces when we get lost.

Finding the Light in the Tunnel

I've found if you don't learn how to work through and heal from your past, it will sooner or later rob you of every good and new thing to enter your life.

My mom and I learned this together, and although we faced a challenging year, we both look back now and see how necessary and transformative it was for our relationship.

As I get older, I've found we aren't as different as I once thought. Some of her mistakes I've experienced as my own mistakes, which makes my love for her stronger, as my mom and as my friend. Today, she is my favorite wine buddy, laughing buddy, and concert buddy. She's protective of me, and I'm protective of her.

Sometimes we get stuck on memory lane, bringing up past pain we both experienced from the divorce and my dad. However, I'm glad to say we're now able to get unstuck and see things from a bird's-eye view.

We're able to see the beauty in the pain, what we learned, how we grew, and where we are now because of what happened then. But this didn't come instantly. It came from years of waiting impatiently and being confused and upset more often than not. It came from wrestling with hard questions and not having the solution to make things better. But we weathered the storm and later saw we were never alone.

You see, no one is ever thankful for trauma in the thick of it, yet what we can learn from our trauma as we heal is it doesn't dictate our future and it does not define us.

I still don't believe everything happens for a reason, but I do believe in time we can find acceptance and peace in complicated and ugly circumstances. I also believe peace comes from faith in God, even when keeping faith is hard.

It's true there is always a light at the end of the tunnel, even if finding the light takes years of staying strong and trying to see a more beautiful place than the one you're in. What I've learned also is there is always a Light in the tunnel, leading you through that dark place and guiding you home.

CHAPTER 3

UNMET EXPECTATIONS

———

"If forgiveness is about releasing, then the opposite of forgiveness means that I'm still holding on. I'm in prison. You're not forgiving to stay safe, but really you're locked up."

— CHRISTIAN DAWSON[13]

Last summer I was staying with my dad and his wife, Andrea, in their new home. It was late afternoon, and he had a surprise for me. I knew surprises weren't ever as neat as my dad built them up to be, yet I played along and went upstairs to get ready. Andrea came in a few moments later and hinted I'd better wear a swimsuit.

When I went outside, my dad was pulling his blue, freshly painted '67 Chevelle out of the garage and then pointed to the driver's seat and said, "You're driving." That afternoon, we drove up to one of his favorite lakes. He stayed by the car

---

13 Christian Dawson, "You Wouldn't Understand," August 23, 2020, in *Bridgetown Audio Podcast*, produced by Bridgetown Church, Podcast, MP3 audio, 44:00.

and had a beer at the top of the hill we parked on while I went for a swim down below.

Afterward, he told me to pull into the A&W park n' eat. We each got a sundae and shared a small fry. He talked to a local about cars while we ate, and I posted a picture of our outing on my Instagram story. To end our trip, we checked out a thrift store.

Before going in, my dad looked to the left and noticed a bar with multiple signs prohibiting guns and, of course, begged me to go inside so he could let it be known *he* was carrying a gun. He told me he didn't like the guy who owned the place and wanted to see what he would do when he walked in.

I felt like a parent telling their kids they can't have a candy bar again and again while waiting in line at the grocery store, but I finally got my dad into the thrift store and away from starting problems.

I got a cool mug that day and then we went home. Now, I'm not the biggest car person and could have cared less about driving his Chevelle, but I can't lie and say I didn't enjoy seeing the smile on my father's face every time I revved the engine or we got looks from other people as we drove through town.

He was proud of all the work he had done on his car, and most of all, he was proud to have me right there next to him, something we both never thought possible.

Everything I mentioned above was my dad's idea—the drive, the swim, the ice cream, the thrift store, and even the attempt to start problems. It wasn't my ideal surprise, but for him, it was a massive gesture to let me know he cares.

I spent most of my childhood dreaming up afternoons like this with my dad, and those dreams dissipated as I grew older because I began accepting they might not ever happen. What set this day and other recent experiences apart is over time I've grown to love my dad for who he is, not for who I wish he was.

I want to share more of our history, but I should first let you know we are at a much better place than we once were.

Knowing the relationship dynamic I have with my dad is important because over the years it has greatly influenced how I handle emotion, how I see myself, and where I still struggle.

I want to share these things with you because through my own story, I've come to recognize the powerful role relationships play in our overall health and wellbeing.

For instance, when we hold a grudge against someone for years on end, we put ourselves at risk for things like chronic stress. As a professor of mine once put it, "If you get stuck in threatened thinking, you get stuck in the stress response."[14] Chronic stress can reveal itself in many ways, some of which

---

14   Claire Michaels Wheeler, *10 Simple Solutions to Stress: How to Tame Tension & Start Enjoying Life* (Oakland: New Harbinger Publication, 2007), 8.

include: enhanced cardiovascular reactivity, muscle tension, headaches, fatigue, restlessness, insomnia, depression, and anxiety.[15]

The good news is we don't have to live in a stress-induced state forever. One of the ways we can move forward is by cultivating secure relationships through both time and forgiveness, which is what I hope to show you next.

Searching for Love

As a kid, I always looked forward to Saturdays because it was the day my dad and I got up early while my mom and brother stayed asleep. I got to pick out my outfit and go to the grocery store with him and only him, two things I found special.

Before going into the store, my dad would always say, "Now listen, I don't want you asking me for anything when we go in here. I have stuff to do today. We are going to be in and out." Looking back, I think this was more of a pep talk for himself. Something about my dad was memorable, and it didn't matter where we went, he was constantly starting up conversations with people in our small town.

I wasn't bothered by this as much as I was bothered by not being able to take a box of Cookie Crisp home *just one Saturday*. It was always a choice between Honey-Nut Scooters, Fruit Spins, Apple Dapples, Marshmallow Mateys, or Golden Puffs. To ask for anything more would risk being left at home

---

15   Wheeler, *10 Simple Solutions to Stress*, 9.

the following week. So, I'd savor my free cookie from the bakery and follow closely behind my dad.

Even though I often felt ignored by him as a child, I still cherished our time together because it was scarce. He was a good dad before the divorce and did things my mom didn't always think to prioritize, yet sometimes he made me feel bad for being me—silly and shy with a wild imagination and neediness for both of my parents' attention. Although these things aren't uncommon for a child, he made me feel they were.

Because I received so much of the love, support, and encouragement I needed as a kid from my mom, I didn't realize how absent these nurturing characteristics were in my relationship with my father until after the divorce when they were no longer there. Parts of him I had never seen before were revealed, and the child in me had a hard time accepting a love so transactional and bare.

After being granted full custody, he had no idea how to be a parent, and by the way he treated my brother and me, it didn't always seem like he wanted to be one. When it came time to be present and take care of us, he lacked the skills.

He didn't know how to get us ready for school or how to talk to us when we were having a bad day. He didn't know how to help with homework, or how to position the night light, or turn on the radio and crack the door just right after tucking me in. He didn't know how to tuck me in. He didn't know how to be a dad without a mom there to help. He didn't know how to love. *He just didn't know.*

And I felt this lack of knowledge every day.

It seemed my dad viewed being a parent as more practical than relational, like making sure there was a roof over our head, food on the table, and we had essentials like a few pairs of clothes, some shoes, a bed, and occasional—but not too much—fun. When it came to things like physical touch, talking about feelings, affirming words, and other basic nurturing patterns, I rarely felt the love of my father.

I thought love came in the form of service, and when I got older, I thought that service was something I had to pay for to receive.

From the age of nine, I was home alone often and would try to stay busy to avoid my monsters reminding me I was alone. If my dad hadn't left me a chore list already, I would spend time vacuuming, doing laundry, yard work, and anything else to perfect the environment around me.

I'll never forget the afternoon I dusted each individual blind within every window. These things made me feel safe, and in doing them, I felt more in control of my current situation.

At the same time, I thought maybe if I did things "right," my dad would notice me. Not just notice me but love me.

In her bestseller *Girl, Wash Your Face*, Rachel Hollis echoes this belief when talking about her childhood: "When I succeeded, I got praise and attention; I felt liked and accepted.

But the moment the audience stopped clapping, it all went back to the way it was before."[16]

The belief that *in order to be loved, I must produce something* followed her into adulthood and led to a poor relationship with work, which also echoes much of what I struggle with now. She says, "The second I achieve one goal, and I mean, the second it's accomplished, I immediately think, *Okay, what next?* I struggle to celebrate or enjoy any victory, no matter how big, because I'm always mindful of something bigger I could be doing instead."[17]

My dad bought a bar immediately following the divorce and started serial dating, which only made me believe my monsters more. *I am alone. I am forgotten.* I constantly felt second to the women he'd come stumbling in the door with after a heavy night of drinking. Out of all of them, only three lasted longer than the expiration date of the milk in our refrigerator. However, I will spare you the details because it would require writing a whole other book.

What I will say is some of them were better than others, and some were worse than them all. Nevertheless, none of them were my mom, and I hated when they pretended they were.

The emotional abuse my dad inflicted on me through his actions made it—and sometimes still does make it—hard to be happy for him.

---

16   Rachel Hollis, *Girl, Wash Your Face* (Nashville, Thomas Nelson, 2018), 22.
17   Ibid.

I have to remind myself I've already forgiven him.

For keeping me from my mom and lying to me in an attempt to "protect me."
For being more focused on sex and alcohol than he was on me and my brother.
For making me take a cab to basketball practice so he could go to the bar.
For not spending time with me and still pretending he knew me.
For being verbally abusive and using words as weapons.

One of the reasons forgiveness is so challenging in my relationship with my dad is because I've never truly felt heard by him.

From a young age, I learned it wasn't worth it to express emotion. When I tried, I was mocked, laughed at, called an annoying nickname (McGillicutty, Vern, Carlos), or not taken seriously at all. It was easier for me to slide under the radar than to deal with him making fun of me or getting defensive when I tried to tell him how I felt.

My suppressed emotions eventually led me to believe that because my dad made me *feel* less than, I *was* less than. This behavior carried on into other relationships throughout my teenage and adult years, and through my healing journey, I've had to relearn how to express emotion and trust I will be safe when I do.

Author and church leader Danny Silk sums it up well when he writes, "People who cannot trust will not show the truth of what is going on inside them to anyone. They feel safer keeping the 'broken spot' concealed. It takes a safe place to expose a vulnerable place, an area that needs healing."[18]

What activated my limbic system more than anything was when other people told me how proud my dad was of me, expanding on what little information he had of my success in school and sports, and making it seem as if he was right there to witness it all.

My dad doesn't deserve bragging rights!
He doesn't even know what is going on in my life!
The only thing he is proud of is his ability to stand and take credit for who I am, even though who I am has been an attempt to be everything he isn't.
If he was proud of me, maybe he should tell me himself. That's all I've ever wanted.

I'm happy my father and I have started to mend the brokenness of our relationship, yet it's hard to forget memories that have left deep wounds.

Nights I'd come home from sporting events and find my dad on the couch with a beer in his hand after telling me he'd try to make it.

Nights he came into my room after arriving home from the bar to tell me he was sorry for not being a better dad and was going to turn himself into a treatment center to get help for his alcohol addiction, and then never did.

---

18 Danny Silk, *Culture of Honor: Sustaining a Supernatural Environment* (Shippensburg: Destiny Image Publishers, 2009), 182.

All the tears, apologies, and hugs forgotten.

As an adult, I struggle to pick up the phone when my dad calls because I know when I do, three things are likely to happen:

1. He will be intoxicated, repeating himself and forgetting a majority of what we spoke about later.
2. He will talk for the length of our phone call, asking me very little about my life.
3. Without knowing me or understanding me, he will critique the things I'm doing and the choices I'm making, discarding the fact I'm now an adult and know some things about life I didn't use to.

My dad gets upset because I never answer the phone, and I get upset he never listens to me.

He once called me as I was walking into a yoga class and I decided to pick up.

"Hey, Dad, I can't talk long because I'm about to head into a yoga class."

"Yoga? Okay, well, I just realized I've never asked you what you're studying in school."

At this point, I didn't care if I was late for class. I was a senior in college and had been waiting the last four years for him to ask me this question.

However, as I began telling him about my major and the path I was on, I found his biggest concern was knowing how much money I'd be making.

"You're damn smart, Carly, you shouldn't let your college degree go to waste."

Ignoring the comments that didn't serve me, I clung to the ones that did. I held tight to the fact my dad was trying. He was doing his best.

Only, the next time I saw him, he had completely forgotten about having this conversation and when I asked him if he had been drinking, he laughed and said, "Yeah, I had a few drinks that day."

On my twenty-third birthday, he called and in an hour and a half told me about the new car he bought, the new job he was about to start, and his dream to become a motivational speaker. But I think his hope to be a motivational speaker is less about motivating and more about him talking. He's told me before the reason why he loves singing karaoke so much is because he loves attention.

I have so many memories of my dad running karaoke for our family with his stereo system at family barbeques and weddings. I'd sing Shania Twain's "Man! I Feel Like a Woman" with my cousins and we'd dance around the yard, watermelon dripping from our chins and dirt collecting on the bottoms of our feet. In between our shenanigans, it wasn't unusual for him to sing one or two songs.

I'll never forget when I was in high school and he got up and sang Lynyrd Skynyrd's "Simple Man" at the top of his lungs in front of crowds of people sitting on both sides of Main Street during one of our town's annual parades.

I still remember being flushed with the brightest hue of red when I first heard my dad's confident, out-of-tune vocals, reaching for notes his voice was nowhere near equipped to handle. I wanted to hide under a rock and never show my face in the halls of my high school ever again after that experience.

Ask me what my most embarrassing moment is, and at age twenty-three, this is the first thing that pops into my head—after six years.

See, my dad loves attention so much he often forgets to give it to those around him who need it most. If it doesn't involve him or if he doesn't have anything to say, he doesn't want to talk about it.

For too long, I interpreted this as *I'm not important and he doesn't care about me.*

Do you know that feeling? I think it's safe to say we all have people in our lives like this and trying to navigate a healthy relationship with boundaries takes loads of strength, patience, and prayer.

Part of me has always wondered if my father's need for attention is similar to mine. Is it something he craves because it's something he didn't have enough of growing up? These big-picture moments are what have made forgiveness more within reach—both forgiveness toward others and toward me.

The Breaking Point

There are many things in life one can deem as trauma, and what is traumatic to an individual is understood best by the Three E's: Events, Experience, and Effects.[19] My trauma was not caused by a single event. Rather, repeated occurrences over time inhibited my ability to process emotion or cope healthily.

I'd avoid being home at all costs because home was not home. It was a lot of beer cans, cuss words, and strangers smoking cigarettes on my front porch. It was my stepsister and new boyfriends. It was fighting, passive-aggressiveness, and aggressiveness. It was being asked to pick up my dad and his friends from the bar.

All of these things and more I constantly tried to escape through different distractions like men, obsession over what I was eating and how much I was exercising, school, extracurriculars, cleaning, organizing, writing, filling my schedule with as many to-do's possible, and a whole lot of Jesus.

It's hard to be a teenager when you feel like you've been an adult for the majority of your life. It's hard to be present when you've been living two steps ahead for so long. You start to

19   "MSN Course Insight: The Three 'E's' of Trauma Every Nurse Practitioner Should Know," Walden University, accessed September 3, 2020.

fear the world collapsing in on you every time the thought to slow down or take a break arises.

Switching from a carefree, bubbly teenager who did normal teenage things to having to be a responsible, mature voice of reason in my life was exhausting.

I wanted to be able to hang out at the mall or other public spaces like a parking lot just for fun (since that seemed to be a trend in high school). I wanted to go to more sporting games and events instead of doing homework, cleaning up the house, and running errands. I wanted to talk and laugh about nothing. I think I probably even wanted to gossip.

Instead, I judged my peers for doing these things because for me, they did not come naturally and seemed immature, irresponsible, and a waste of time.

Eventually, my relationship with my father hit a breaking point, and I fought harder than I ever have to get out of his home. The result of this was both beautiful and ugly. I had no contact with him and his family for close to three years, and it was weighty accepting he or his parents might not ever be a part of my life again.

When I look back at high school graduation photos now, all I can see is a frail and weak girl hurting, pretending like the absence of her dad and grandparents that day didn't bother her.

I will give the full story of these events later on in the book.

Reconciliation

Toward the middle of my freshman year of college, my dad and I met up for dinner, and it was an absolute train wreck. He showed up late, drunk, and sobbing because Andrea broke off the wedding they had planned.

The words from his mouth were: "I just lost everything that ever meant something to me."

I was fuming with hatred. It had been two and a half years since I'd seen my dad, and I'd worried myself sick up until that point, spending way too long to get ready because I wanted him to see how grown up I was. I wanted him to be reminded of how much he had missed.

I have more compassion for this moment now, but at the time all I could think was how stupid I was for thinking our relationship might actually be different, for thinking my dad might actually be different.

The second attempt to reconnect with him was better, especially after having time in between to cool down.

I joined my dad, grandparents, uncle, and a few of my cousins for dinner after not being around them in nearly three years, and although I was nervous, it ended up being another small step toward forgiveness with my family.

No date
My dad was the same old, same old. Most of the time, he talked about himself and all of the women who "want" him. The rest

of the time, he talked about how he wants to change. I think he might be telling the truth this time, it's just so hard for me to believe the things he says. It was nice, however, to hear him say four things I've wanted to hear for a long time:

1. *He told me he's thinking about getting help because he wants to be able to meet his grandchildren. He knows he won't ever get that opportunity if he continues down the path he's on.*
2. *He said he was hurt in the past and is going to stop being bitter and try harder to mend our relationship.*
3. *He said I looked pretty tonight.*
4. *He owned up to his drinking problem and said it's only gotten worse since Andrea left.*

I love my dad, and I miss him. I hope this step is one that's going forward and not backward. I love my grandparents too. It was nice to be in their company tonight and to hear their voices. Although it was awkward at times, I believe the dinner we had is one of the biggest steps we could've all taken toward forgiveness. Grandpa has prostate cancer and quite honestly, I think it is partly his illness that's worked to bring us all closer. We're beginning to see just how precious life is and most of all, how important family is.

If it weren't for believing God was bigger than the adversity with family, these circumstances would've seemed much worse. But He was at work in the background of it all. Similar to the story of my mom, I didn't completely see it at the time, but He was doing several things to align us all on the path toward healing and forgiveness.

Forgiving Isn't Forgetting

I know I've spent the last little bit speaking to some of the more negative encounters with my dad, and again, things between him and I are so much better than they once were.

What I will say is my dad won't agree with everything I've written here, nor will he agree with all that took place when I left his home. That's okay because we experienced the events differently and were both uniquely affected.

But I want to make something clear: my dad hasn't changed, my perspective has.

In late 2017, I received a Facebook message from Andrea letting me know that in less than a week, she and my dad were getting married (for real, this time) and I was invited.

Although it was an odd way to let people know about a wedding, and it was super short notice, I ended up going with two friends by my side. The whole night they were asking me if I was okay, and when I responded with "yes," I wasn't lying.

I *was* happy for them.

Once I started to grasp the power of forgiveness, it all clicked. I've learned forgiveness is not so much about the other person, it's about you. It's about setting yourself free from something that has been eating you alive. It's about moving on and choosing to let go.

Forgiving doesn't mean you have to forget what happened. You can still set boundaries with the person who hurt you to protect yourself from similar events happening again, and you may have to forgive more than once because forgiveness is not a one-time thing.

I've forgiven my dad hundreds of times, and each time I see or talk to him, I have to do it again. Because deep down, that small child in me wants more of her father.

This is true of both my parents.

I know now my dad was only doing his best, and like most people, he has his own trauma to deal with.

The more I've learned about his past, the more I've seen the small child in him too, the one crying out for something missing.

You might have parents or people in your life who've disappointed you. If that's the case, I'm sorry. I know it doesn't always make sense and it hurts, but I want to challenge you to think about the resentment you still carry toward those people.

What would it look like to move on from that resentment?

For me, it meant focusing on where I was carrying burdens that weren't mine to carry. It meant long counseling sessions where I learned how to name my feelings and accept them, times when I cried out to God and eventually understood

His love and care for me far exceeded the abilities of my earthly father.

It won't always make sense to forgive and rarely will it come naturally, yet I'm confident with each small step and with every chain broken, you will gain more freedom, ease, and joy in your life.

Forgiving my dad showed me he didn't have as much power over me as I once thought. It taught me how to stop pointing the blame and believe I was worthy, even if he never told me it himself. I became healthier because my load got lighter. My anger subsided, and I had more energy, time, and love in my heart.

Don't you want that? To feel free and know regardless of the things that go wrong in your life or the people who fail to show up, you are loved and cherished?

The good news is you can and you will.

If you look to God and let Him gaze back at you, you will find your needs and aches are satisfied. You can slow down and trust you're taken care of and loved.

CHAPTER 4

BULLIES TO BUDDIES

———

Help me God, to remain steadfast when under trial, counting it all as joy and remembering that the testing of faith is what produces steadfastness and that after standing the test, I will receive the crown of life.

I had four holes in my door when I was younger from different times I pushed my older brother's buttons a little too far. He would chase me to my room, bang on my door, and scream at the top of his lungs whenever I was quick enough to make it to my room before he did. It was not unusual for me to call my dad at work crying because "He won't stop being mean!"

My brother did a lot of things when we were younger that hurt me both physically and emotionally. However, I now see the humor in each event and have grace for the bored, broken kids we were.

I remember one day we got home from the store and he was in the backyard shooting the eyes of my favorite baby doll out with his paintball gun because I had done something to upset him. Once he took my barbie doll from me, and every time I made a noise, he would slowly, inch by inch, dip the barbie's entire body into his cereal bowl and laugh.

When we were up before our parents one morning, he was jumping from the couch to the ottoman and I wanted to try, too. I was surprised when he finally did let me try, but as I leaped from the couch and spread my arms out to land face down on the ottoman, my loving brother thought it would be funny to pull the cushion off and I landed on an assortment of old wood and creaky springs. The rest of that morning was spent in the emergency room.

More than once, he would make me scratch his back or give him a massage before he agreed to make lunch, which usually consisted of a grilled cheese or Top Ramen. He would pour cold water on me in the shower, lock me out of the house, and trick me into eating gross jellybeans or thought-up concoctions.

I had fun teasing him just as much as he had fun teasing me. When he started dating his high school girlfriend, she would frequently come over to our house. My dad would make them leave the door open, and whenever they went to put on a movie, I'd ask if I could watch it, too. My brother would automatically say no and tell me to leave, but I wasn't ever good at taking no for an answer.

So, I'd sit in the hallway, exactly on the line of where the carpet changed color, watching the movie (more so watching my brother burn with anger) from the doorway, smiling. He'd yell at me to get out of his room, and I'd assure him, "I'm not in your room. I'm in the hallway."

While living with my dad's parents after the divorce, there was one afternoon when my brother told me not to ride his bike over to the neighbors or I'd be sorry. So, what did I do? Well, of course, I shook my head and told him okay to his face. Then I waited until the coast was clear and made my way over to his bike, got on it, and started pedaling down the gravel hill of my grandparents' driveway.

Within seconds, I saw him dart out from under the porch to chase me, and instead of stopping the bicycle, I pedaled even faster. Before I knew it, I was flying over the handlebars like an acrobat, sliding against gravel with barely any clothing on to protect me.

Keep in mind, this was only a few days before my first day of school in the fifth grade. I'll never forget showing up with a scabbed-over face and body because of my stubbornness to not be caught by my brother's quickstep and rage. Seeing what I could do to rile him up when we were kids was a hobby. He, on the other hand, was a full-time specialist in the department of sibling rivalry.

I knew he had anger issues, and it was fun for me to test them, yet he knew I was sensitive and was skilled at targeting my weaknesses and executing his plans to make me upset. My plans sometimes worked, while his plans always worked.

When I was younger, I loved the band TLC. My mom had gifted me their CD and I'd play it over and over. I played all of my CDs over and over—the Dixie Chicks, Britney Spears, and *so much* Taylor Swift. I would take the little CD cover out of the case and follow along with the lyrics, singing at the top of my lungs.

Sometimes, instead of using the boom box in my bedroom, I'd play the CDs on my Walkman and sing out loud with headphones on. If my brother was bothered by it or I knew someone was listening, I'd sing even louder. My younger sister used to do this and, wow, I'm still so sorry for everyone who had to listen to that.

My brother has always been savvy with anything media-related, and when my TLC CD got scratched and started skipping one day, I asked him, "Hey, what's that trick you always do when your DVDs have scratches?"

He was very simple in his reply. "You set it on a paper towel, rub butter on it, and put it in the microwave for thirty seconds." The way he described the process was so matter of fact I didn't even question his advice. *Of course, butter and a microwave are how you get scratches out of CDs. Why didn't I know that?*

Just a fair warning: butter and a microwave are not how you get scratches out of CDs. Butter and a microwave are how you get *rid* of a CD. He stood at the counter while I followed his instructions, smiling and being overly nice. Just when I thought I might tell him thank you, I heard sparks exploding from the microwave and him laughing loudly.

That was the last day I ever played my TLC CD, a sad, sad day for me, and a brilliant day for my brother. However, his glory days didn't last long because eventually, I got over TLC and was perfectly satisfied with my new Avril Lavigne CD.

Closer through Adversity

My parents' divorce brought my brother and me much closer than we were before, and although we still fought and bickered, we always had each other's backs. One evening, we ran away on our bikes when we couldn't stand my dad, missed our mom, and wanted nothing more than to be out of our current situation. He brought bread, a knife, and peanut butter and jelly from the kitchen in his backpack, and we sat on the edge of a bike trail in the forest nearby while we ate our dusty, soggy sandwiches and tried to plan our next move.

Eventually, we ventured back home from the forest. I can't remember what caused us to ditch our runaway plan that evening, yet I do remember being comforted by the realization that he understood what I was feeling just as much as I understood what he was feeling.

We wanted our family back. We were tired of staying at strangers' homes and strangers staying in our home, but because my dad was also hurting, he paid little attention to how we both were coping.

My brother was gone as much as possible after the divorce. He coped by hanging out with his friends, smoking, drinking, skipping school, skateboarding, and listening to music.

I, on the other hand, was too young to just leave whenever I wanted and had a tighter leash around my neck.

Aside from cleaning, listening to music, and journaling, I have very little recollection of how I spent my time coping early after the divorce. Most days when I was alone, all I remember doing was waiting for my dad or brother to get home.

Even though my brother and I were not the closest of friends, something about his presence made me feel safe. Just having him in the house when our dad was gone relieved my wandering mind and worry.

It was always a special day for me when my brother would ask to go somewhere and would only be allowed if he brought me with him. I'd tag along to his girlfriend's house, to the park, to the river—I really didn't care as long as I didn't have to be home.

One night, he brought me to a house party and though I was neither interested nor old enough to drink, I still played beer pong with his friend nicknamed Rhino, who drank my beverages for me.

I have many memories, going places and doing things I probably shouldn't have done at such a young age. However, I'm glad to say most of these things didn't negatively impact me the way some were worried they would. The truth is, I observed the outcome of a lot of poor decisions around me when I was younger, and I didn't want to repeat those decisions as I got older.

I think this is probably why in high school my brother got all sappy one day and said he was proud of me. He said I was accomplishing all the things he wished he would have done. He was happy I didn't follow in his footsteps because he had always been the screw-up, and I had always been the overachiever to rise above the adversity we faced as kids. "At least one of us turned out good," he told me.

When I look back on that day, I wish I could have told him something comforting in return. I didn't want him to feel like his life didn't matter because I had chosen to live mine differently. Yet, I know it is a common pattern in families for siblings to compare themselves to each other because I do it, too.

There are a lot of things about my brother I wished I could've replicated when I was younger, his love for other people being one of them. If I could go back to that day, I would remind him of all the things he's taught me, like how he taught me to be strong.

He showed me how to make the best out of the cards we were dealt and has this beautiful ability to not critique people like I often do but to accept them for all of their wrongdoings. He is a great forgiver, especially when it comes to our dad.

During my eating disorder, I never once felt judged by my brother. He'd make jokes about how healthy I ate and often when I was obsessing over a food choice, he'd tell me to stop stressing because, "It's just food, Carly."

My Great Protector

My brother moved out soon after he graduated from high school. If it weren't for my dad's controlling behavior and his love for me, he would have moved out sooner, except he promised my mom he would stay a little while longer to make sure I was okay.

My mom feared what would happen when he was no longer there with me, just as much as I did. If anyone ever decided to lay a hand on me, I knew he would be right there to keep me safe, which is why I never felt unprotected when he was around. However, I cannot blame him for leaving and was glad when he finally did move out, he still came over to check on me.

He knew his role in our family, which was to be strong and stand up for things that were wrong. For this reason, it was not uncommon for me to watch my brother and dad fistfight. Several times, I was held in the arms of whoever my dad was dating at the time while he had my brother in a chokehold and I watched his face turn blue.

Very seldom did arguments between them end without notes of blood and marks of pain. Nothing hurt me more than to watch them fight, but I was thankful because my brother always took the worst of our dad's anger and drunkenness.

On nights when I was home alone and scared, or when my dad would come stumbling in from the bar with a woman he had met that night, I'd call him unable to catch my breath from the rush of emotions I was experiencing.

I'd make my bed on the couch and cry, trying to block out the noise of my father giving in to his sexual desires and loudly entertaining women right next to my bedroom, sometimes with the door open. I would remember the days when my dad's room wasn't just a place for him to mess around with strangers but a haven for my mother and father to express their love and to rest in each other's arms.

My brother would come in through the front door, angry and amazed by my dad's selfishness, while also tender-hearted and caring toward me. He'd brush my hair back or give me a hug to try and calm me down on the couch before—without hesitation—bursting through my father's door and yelling at him for the stupidity of his actions.

He would distract me in moments like this by giving me hope, and lots of it.

"Only a few more years," he'd say. "I know it's hard now, but soon enough, you will have a decision and be able to leave."

But it wasn't just a few more years for me. It was five more years. Five more years of being an adult before I even hit adulthood. Five more years of living with my dad and not actually feeling like I had one. Thankfully, I didn't have to stick out those five years and was able to leave sooner than expected, another event where my brother was a major support for me.

One of the things I find hard to put into words is my relationship with my dad, and what I love most about my brother is that I don't have to. Because he went through a lot of the same stuff I did, he's always understood and acknowledged my frustration.

Making the Best of What You're Given

Today, my brother and I don't talk too often because we live a couple of hours apart. Yet, it's not hard for us to pick up where we left off and bond over things, no matter how big or small. Small things being music and movies, and big things being relationships and past or present pains.

My dad hasn't made it to a lot of the important events in my life thus far, but my older brother almost always has. I'll never forget him carrying my heavy dresser up six flights of stairs the day I moved into the dorms of Portland State. He carried several other heavy belongings that day I could have never lifted myself, and he did it all with a positive attitude and excitement for the adventure in front of me.

He's forever been one of my biggest supporters who I know I can trust and confide in. At times, he's been a father figure to me, and at other times, I've had to be a mother figure to him. We didn't come from a perfect family, but we worked with what we were given and made many memories in the mess of it all.

If it weren't for our parents' divorce, there's a good chance he and I wouldn't be nearly as close as we are now, and although nobody ever wishes to go back and repeat history, I think we're both thankful for what came from hard times.

Most of all, we're both thankful for where we are now, for Marley and Linkin entering our lives, for no longer being separated from our mom, for having an okay relationship with our dad, and for accomplishing what we have as individuals.

Count It All Joy

In the last three chapters, I have described my relationship with my mom, dad, and brother. What I hoped to convey in each chapter was this:

I love my mom, but it's taken me a long time to release the resentment I've had toward her in my heart. Most of all, it's taken a long time to accept what happened in the past and find peace.

I love my dad, but there are things he did that hurt me and caused painful events in my life. I've had to release him from my resentment, too, by learning the power of forgiveness.

I also love my brother, but there have been times I've sworn I hated him. I haven't always appreciated his existence as I do now and know the obstacles I faced and am still facing would be much more difficult without him here.

Over the years, these things have shaped me in ways I'm still trying to figure out.

I think about how my mother and father's absence have, throughout my life, changed the way I view myself, how their words have lessened my trust and made it seem as if I'm carrying the world on my shoulders.

How did growing up without my mother's beauty influence the way I see myself?

How did my father's words change the way I speak to myself?

How did my brother's undesired behavior impact my perfectionistic behavior?

Did our fights and the things we look back and laugh at now possess more power than we thought? Was my attempt to push his buttons to the point of an angry outburst derived from a motive to make my dad notice and love me more?

It's all connected.

To express the relationships, memories, and events of my childhood and how they have affected me up to this point is not an attempt to live in the past. Instead, it is a way for me to showcase the many layers I spoke of earlier and how they relate to the eating disorder I battled, as well as how they relate to the feeling of never being enough.

It's a reminder for you—the reader—that sometimes you have to go through the storm before you can see the rainbow.

It is only recently in my life I've started to see the rainbow, and now I want to help you find your own rainbow.

To end, I want to share a passage from the book of James that resonates with me. I hope you too, find it reassuring in the difficult moments you find yourself in.

"Count it all joy, my brothers, when you meet trials of various kinds, for you know that the testing of your faith produces steadfastness. And let steadfastness have its full effect, that you may be perfect and complete, lacking in nothing."[20]

---

20 James 1:2-4 (English Standard Version).

CHAPTER 5

CHASING ACCEPTANCE

——

"If we want to fully experience love and belonging, we must believe we are worthy of love and belonging."

—BRENÉ BROWN[21]

When I was younger, one of my best friends was a girl named Mary. We met on the school bus one morning and were practically inseparable after. She was nearly two years older than me, however, most of my close friends were older than me at that time.

My neighbor, Chay, was also two years older than me. She taught me how to wear eyeliner and stuff my bra on nights we'd go to the skating rink and flirt with boys who had long, shaggy hair and holes in their jeans. Chay also showed me some old VHS tapes containing porn that her parents had hidden.

---

21 Brené Brown, *The Gifts of Imperfection: Let Go of Who You Think You're Supposed to Be and Embrace Who You Are* (Center City: Hazelden Publishing, 2010), 23.

Mary and Chay lived in average homes, and I wasn't afraid to have them over because of their own stories of pain and brokenness. I didn't have to hide anything from them, which is why they were the only friends I invited over after the divorce.

I tended to keep my home life hidden from everyone at school because I was embarrassed, embarrassed our house wasn't what it once was before and embarrassed not much of our furniture matched. I was embarrassed it was often freezing during the fall and winter days until a fire was built in the evening, embarrassed I didn't have much food to offer, and embarrassed because I lived with my dad and brother and no longer had a mom.

Unlike the judgment I felt from others, Mary and Chay never viewed my home life as unusual. They felt like equals. We laughed at similar things and found joy in scrounging up any change we could find just to buy a Slurpee or some beef jerky sticks from across the road.

We'd find contentment in the small things, like hanging out and listening to music or watching a movie. At that age, twenty dollars felt like the equivalent to winning the lottery, and getting to do anything that wasn't wandering around outside or complaining about how we were bored was a privilege.

A few of the most exciting moments I had with Mary were the day we made a Myspace account, the day we tried piercing my nose, and the day we threw a party out in the shop at her house.

With Chay, a few standout moments I remember are the day we made Hotmail accounts (mine was luv-carly12@hotmail.com, and I made it when I was eleven), the day her dad set up a tetherball pole in their front yard, and another time her mom let us blow up a kiddie pool in the backyard on a hot summer day. We'd take turns swinging on the hammock and sitting in the pool because it wasn't big enough for the both of us.

All of these marks of accomplishment were small but felt massive at the time. Big moments in what felt like our tiny, tiny world.

It was comforting to have my older friends around until I'd have to go to school, and they were either in a different classroom or in an entirely different school.

After my parents' divorce, I dealt with small amounts of bullying and, without my friends being there, it made going to school even more dreadful. Once, there was a rumor spread in fifth grade that I was pregnant, and on another occasion, a group of girls thought it would be funny to pour water over all the books in my cubby.

The worst part is I never stood up for myself, and even though I often went home crying and hated how I was treated, I *still* felt the need to please a lot of people (mostly girls) who were rude to me. I internalized their snide comments and glares as flaws and did everything I could to try and win acceptance.

These moments made having Mary and Chay helpful. I never told them the hurtful details of the girls at school, but I'd observe how they dressed and acted. I thought if I could mimic them, maybe then I would fit in.

I've obsessed over how other people see me from a young age, and it started after my mom left and was unable to build me up and love me as she did before. I had so much doubt surrounding my every move, including minuscule things like the clothes on my body.

I wanted to know how to do my hair in ways not involving a big wet bun slicked back on top of my head, and I wished the kids at school would quit calling me "monkey" and "gorilla" because of the thick blond hairs on my arms and legs.

The constant message that lingered was, *You are not good enough.*

The reason I felt I wasn't good enough was because my family was no longer put together and, instead, was scattered and broken.

I did have a couple of friends in elementary school who were in my grade and made me feel accepted, friends who I would play tetherball with every day at recess and sit with at assemblies.

These friends were still close to the girls who didn't like me. Still, it never stopped them from saying hello or choosing to sit with me at lunch. When we were together, they'd tell me they didn't understand why the other girls didn't like me, and I should just ignore them.

A weird, twisted part of me was always curious to know what the mean girls were saying behind my back, but one friend, in particular, was always thoughtful to protect me from facing even more disappointment and letdown than I already had.

Before too long, we were heading off to middle school, anyway. I'd make new friends who liked me for who I was. One of the staff members in elementary school was constantly reminding me, "They might be on the top now, but before too long they'll go off to middle school and be back at the bottom." She didn't like them either, I don't think.

Keeping Hope

When I thought about middle school, I feared being an outsider even more than I already was. I wanted to make a good impression on the first day. So, I asked my dad for extra money to get name brand clothes like all of the other "cool kids." Getting my dad to give me money in the first place was hard enough and to ask for extra money was a long shot. But I had to do it. My reputation was on the line.

I didn't have a ton of clothes after my mom left and I started growing, and I certainly didn't have any name brand ones. So, you can imagine how happy I was coming home with two shirts from Aeropostale, along with two new—not hand-me-down—pairs of jeans from Pac Sun. I wore those four items over and over and over until the balls of cotton became too visible on the shirts and I outgrew the jeans.

By the time I was in middle school, I had one more year with Mary and Chay before they left for high school. For this reason, sixth grade ended up being much better than elementary school. I got to start over with new teachers and kids from other schools who didn't know anything about my past.

I've always felt a need to stick up for the underdogs, and I think it's because I felt like an underdog when I was younger. Looking back, I don't know if the events I recall from elementary school and early middle school days are as troublesome as I've made them out to be, yet at the time they were.

My tears were not fake, and neither were my feelings. I truly felt bullied and alone, and if I would've had a healthy dialogue about these events when I was younger, I don't think they would remain as big a scar now.

My little sister is in middle school, and I've heard stories that instantly bring me back to my story. I worry about her and want to protect her. At the same time, I remember she is already protected because she is not alone. She has a family, Jesus, and me—her big sister who will always be there for her—with no strings attached.

I can't continually compare my story to hers because we are two different people. What I can do, however, is initiate healthy dialogue between us, the same healthy dialogue I needed when I was younger. I can listen to her when she feels like "no one cares," and I can use my story as proof that *things will get better.*

My story keeps me hopeful for not only my sister, but for every other human in need of love and acceptance.

I can relate to them, pray for them, share with them, and dream with them about the turn their story is going to take and the work God is going to do if only they don't lose hope.

That includes you.

Better Than Basketball

When seventh grade arrived, I decided I wanted to play basketball to stay busy. I had grown up playing basketball but stopped when my parents separated and I didn't have the encouragement to continue.

When I told my father I wanted to try out for the seventh-grade travel team, he told me he wouldn't be driving and taking me to all the tournaments and games on the weekends. I promised him he wouldn't have to. If he could just pay, I assured him I'd take care of the rest. I'd find rides to all my practices and games, I'd get my mom to buy my shorts and shoes, and I'd make sure my chores were done every day. After much convincing, he agreed to let me try out, and I made the team.

Basketball in seventh grade was challenging because, unlike most other girls, I didn't stay playing consistently. When my parents divorced, many of the things in my childhood were put on pause for years, including sports.

Practices were embarrassing, and I struggled to keep up. I was very uncoordinated when I was a kid, which didn't help my situation. My tall body and lanky limbs seemed to have a mind of their own and caused me to make something simple for someone else look overwhelmingly hard.

On the night of my first basketball game, I'd managed to organize a ride with Rosie, who I mentioned in an earlier chapter. We weren't close friends at this point; I just knew about her and her family through my parents' friend John and his wife. Throughout the years, I often heard stories of Rosie, her father Paul, her mother Janie, and her two siblings.

At the time, I had no idea the role this family would one day play in my life, and the night they picked me up for our first basketball game was only the start of many more drives spent in the backseat of their red Explorer, always filled with snacks and lots of love.

When Rosie and I started playing basketball together in seventh grade, I decided to take our relationship further than the bench. I say bench and not court because, honestly, she and I spent most games learning how to be the best benchwarmers out there. We stayed positive, cheered others on, talked about the latest Gatorade flavor, and did everything in our power not to throw on our hoodies when all our sweat had dried and left us freezing in the dead of winter.

I called her up one afternoon to see if she wanted to hang out. I still remember the conversation. She was unloading the dishwasher and said, "Yeah, that would be fun." Most of the time when you ask someone to hang out, you invite them over. I, on the other hand, suggested it would probably be best if I came over the upcoming weekend and stayed the night.

My dad didn't question me staying at Janie and Paul's because he knew their family and trusted they were good people. Sometimes when I would go to stay at friends' houses, however, he would make me set up a call with the parents so he could approve. When he did this, I think it was less about how much he trusted me and more about him doing the right thing and looking like a responsible parent.

A New Friend, Home, and Family

When I was younger, I always set out my nicest items of clothing when I was going to stay with a friend—my nicest pants, shirts, underwear, socks, pajamas. I felt I had to put on some kind of facade and show up in my best attire to hide the rags of my life I was afraid of others seeing.

I wanted to be accepted and thought matching clothes and nice items would show I was worthy of such acceptance.

Rosie lived in a gorgeous home and had tons of name brand clothes and stuff I'd always dreamt of having, which only increased my striving. But as I continued to spend more time with her and her family, I began to notice how little they cared about the way I looked and the things I owned.

I didn't have to hurry and put makeup on before showing my face in the morning, and I didn't need all of my outfits planned ahead of time. More often than not, I found myself in Rosie's clothes anyway. She wore a smaller size than I did but frequently opened her closet up to me.

"Feel free to try on whatever you want," she would tell me. Even though I often stretched out her clothes and squeezed into things that didn't fit, she'd still say, "I trust you if you want to borrow or wear anything of mine."

What I came to realize about this family was they trusted and deeply loved me. They welcomed me in just as I was. Soon, I felt like I had a new family to call my own.

I would come home from school with Rosie most days or stay the night after basketball practice, and we'd all sit around the table together. We'd pray, we'd laugh, and we'd listen to each other—such a foreign routine to me.

Everyone would pitch in with dinner, grabbing drinks, getting placemats out, buttering the bread, and lighting candles. Some nights we would even have a circle of gratitude where we listed off the things we were grateful for.

Of course, there were nights when everyone's schedule was different, and dinner was either DIY or leftovers. Still, those nights felt special because even if everyone was arriving home at different times and was busy doing their own thing, everyone still came home. We'd convene at some point by either watching a TV show, chatting in the living room, or visiting the next morning at breakfast.

It was uncomfortable at first, eating with other people. I was so used to eating by myself or not eating dinner at all, and I couldn't manage to take a bite at the appropriate time to avoid getting asked a question right after.

Rosie and her family asked *so many* questions. They wanted to know all about school, what I spent my days doing, and how my home life was. They asked questions, and again, they listened.

"How has middle school been for you?"

"How are your classes going?"

"Is there anything you are having a hard time understanding in school?

"What do you normally spend the evenings doing after practice?"

"What's your favorite meal?"

"Do you and your family have any fun dinner traditions?"

It wasn't until I started getting asked these questions that I felt people actually took an interest in me and wanted to know what was going on in my life. Not only was Rosie's home a safe place for me to lay my head, but it was also a safe place for me to be heard and valued.

Rosie was a friend who, unlike my older friends, introduced me to a more positive life than the one I was living. I saw a brighter path ahead when I thought about our friendship.

With Chay and Mary, there were a lot of things I did that I'm not proud of today. Once they went off to high school, we still spoke often. I remained especially close to Mary, who would fill me in on all the high school drama she was experiencing. I spent a lot of nights over at her house, and as she quickly expanded her network of men, they soon became available to me, too.

Mary set me up on a few blind dates where I lied about my age. I got taken advantage of more than once, was sent too many inappropriate images via text, and did whatever I could to please the people next to me.

I wasn't ready to say goodbye to my older friends just yet because of how close we had become. They didn't quite understand my relationship with Rosie, and I didn't bother telling them much. I was still trying to understand and navigate what exactly was happening, and I didn't entirely believe Rosie was someone who would accept me for who I was. *Will she leave like everyone else?*

It's hard when you are young to set standards and values for yourself when both you and your friends haven't had the best example set before you.

I've always been conscious of right from wrong, yet I had a hard time doing the right thing when many of the people around me were doing the wrong thing. There are certain behaviors I had enough discipline to avoid repeating, but I struggled to hold myself accountable with gray areas and normalized patterns. Being one of the only people in my family who believes in and follows Jesus, I still find this a struggle at times because their moral compass is different than mine.

I can't blame myself, Chay, or Mary for the things we did because we were just trying to get by, fit in, and appear less like the hurt children we were beneath the surface. I am glad, however, Rosie came into my life when she did. Before I met her, there was always something nudging my shoulder and reminding me I was made for more, reminding me Chay and Mary were also made for more.

They may have felt the nudge differently, and maybe they still feel it. For me, it came when I was at parties where alcohol and drugs were present. The nudge kept me from participating in either because I was scarred from how these things had been abused in my family and didn't want them to be a part of my future.

The nudge came when I slathered on makeup and spent hours getting ready. I'd be reminded how I didn't need to cover up and put on a mask. I was beautiful in my own way, and one day I would believe it.

Even though I knew my story would be different, I continued to spend time with people who had opposing priorities because at least they accepted me. I couldn't risk being treated poorly by other girls living a more rich, perfect, and pure life. I learned before how gruesome the shame from those episodes can be.

Rosie, on the other hand, showed me not every popular person with a nice house, money, and married parents is stuck up, shallow, and mean. She was everything but that, and her popularity was based more on the kind way she treated people than how much better off she was.

She showed me there was an alternate, more secure way to live, and she gave me a new crowd to claim.

I didn't want to keep living in the rut I was in, and I don't think I would have changed if it weren't for her loving me unconditionally, holding on to me on my best and worst days. She saw me as Carly, God's beloved, and not as Carly, the daughter of an alcoholic, the girl with no mom, the greedy attention seeker.

Learning from Jesus, through Others

There is a story in the Bible where—during the Last Supper before His death—Jesus gets up from the table to wash the feet of His disciples including Judas, who He knew would later betray Him.

> When He had washed their feet and put on his outer garments and resumed His place, He said to them, "Do you understand what I have done to you? You call me Teacher and Lord, and you are right, for so I am. If I then, your Lord and Teacher, have washed your feet, you also ought to wash one another's feet. For I have given you an example, that you also should do just as I have done to you. Truly, truly, I say to you, a servant is not greater than his master, nor is a messenger greater than the one who sent him. If you know these things, blessed are you if you do them.[22]

---

22   John 13:12-17 (ESV).

This story so perfectly exemplifies how we are to love one another, just as Jesus has loved us, but that doesn't mean it's easy. If anything, it doesn't make sense.

I mean, if we knew we were going to die, how many of us would spend our last hours scrubbing the feet of others? Let alone, the feet of our enemies! I can tell you honestly, there are *plenty* of activities I'd prefer doing.

But what I've learned, and am still learning, is how contagious this kind of love is once you've been on the receiving end of it, and we have *all* been on the receiving end of it. Every day when we—in our humanness—fail to meet perfection in the eyes, there is Jesus, full of grace and mercy, and full of love.

When you grasp the power of that love, extending it to other people who may not deserve it starts to make sense.

Perhaps this is why those who truly resemble characteristics of Jesus are thought to appear as "lights," as different than most.

At least that is how I viewed Rosie's family. I had nothing to offer them and was too broken to fill anyone else's cup the way they were filling mine, yet they continued to do so.

There's a kind of love called "need love" which C.S. Lewis defines in his well-known book *The Four Loves*. "Need love," he says, "relates to the supernatural need we have for both God and each other."[23]

> But in the long run, it is apparent even more so in our growing—for it ought to be growing—awareness that our whole being by its very nature is one vast need; incomplete, preparatory, empty yet cluttered, crying out for Him who can untie things that are now knotted together and tie up things that are still dangling loose.[24]

The other kind of "need love," C.S. Lewis says, is a need for one another, a sort of Charity:

> But God also transforms our need-love for one another, and it requires equal transformation. In reality, we all need at times, some of us at most times, that Charity from others which, being Love Himself in them, loves the unlovable. But this, though a sort of love we need, is not the sort we want. We want to be loved for our cleverness, beauty, generosity, fairness, usefulness.[25]

Jesus sets the example for how we are to love one another by verbally expressing His love, and by physically getting down on the ground to wash and dry the feet of His disciples the night before His death.

---

23 C.S. Lewis, *The Four Loves: An Exploration of the Nature of Love* (Boston: Mariner Books Houghton Mifflin Harcourt, 1960), 129.

24 Lewis, *The Four Loves*, 3.

25 Lewis, *The Four Loves*, 131-132.

Need love, I think, breeds a sort of sacrificial love. It's the least appealing, and the hardest to live out. Giving to those it may not make much sense to give to and loving a brother or sister who may not yet know how to love you back. It's leading by example, and that example is Jesus.

When I was younger, I thought love was something I had to earn, but my friend Rosie and her family taught me love was, instead, something I got to embrace.

Eventually, through my embracing and receiving love, I gained the capacity to meet the needs around me. To get to this place took a long time and did not happen immediately—I'm still learning—but Jesus's example is one that trickled down into my being from one person to the next, first by Jesus, then by my friend.

Anytime you sense your heart becoming hardened, selfishness creeping in, or greed taking over, take a second to read through the gospels. It won't be long before Jesus's character starts to soften your heart, widen your view, and take you to places outside of yourself.

We need Jesus, and we need each other. The two are not independent, and although some seasons we will be more of a charity case than a charity worker, the scriptures and C.S. Lewis remind us both roles hold value and beauty. To need is not a sign of weakness; it's a sign of strength.

Already Accepted

Looking back, I see two very different paths that were in front of me. One road was filled with warnings and dead-end signs, while the other was filled with the unknown and places I'd be required to take risks and trust. Had I not chosen to press into my discomfort and confusion, I know I'd be in a much scarier and different place now.

I could've stayed where I was and possibly now be addicted to drugs or alcohol, pregnant, or even homeless. I doubt I would have stayed in sports, graduated from high school, or gone to college. I probably would have sold my heart to a man who didn't deserve it, and it's likely I would've never dealt with my childhood pain and trauma.

Instead, I chose the other road, a road that has led to more than I ever knew possible. It hasn't been easy—life never is—but I think back and tear up at how grateful I am to have gone the other way. I did things my parents haven't ever done. I chose my education, health, and future over coping device on top of coping device, and I chose Jesus.

I've learned with God there's not a whole lot of planning you can do. I've never been one to like surprises, yet over and over again, He's knocked me off my seat and shown me new ways of thinking, living, and being.

When you choose to surrender all you are up to Jesus, He will not let you down. I found this out gradually through the positive and negative relationships I've had with friends and family, and I've found it in many other desperate times in my life, too.

The truth is, you don't have to try and hide your pain to be accepted, not through layers of makeup, nice clothing, or lies about who you are.

Sooner or later, He will reveal what's underneath those things, and in time, you will learn you are already accepted by the Creator of the universe and He knows you by name. Even when He feels far away, His Spirit is as close to you as the hairs on your head.

He's a great friend and an even better listener.

Where in your life are you hiding? How might you better surrender yourself to God?

CHAPTER 6

A PLACE TO CALL HOME

———

I wish I was better at taking the things I read in the Bible and putting them into action. I want to be content with God and nothing else.

Have you ever heard of a "Chreaster"? You know, those Christians who only show up to church on Christmas and Easter? Well, that was my family for most of my childhood, and it wasn't until I started growing closer with Rosie that I regularly attended church.

I'd find myself over at her home most Saturday nights, which led to being there Sunday mornings when her family would get ready for their weekly church service. Naturally, I began joining them.

Church for me started out as very low-impact. I knew how to distract myself, and when I got bored, I'd doodle on the guest envelope in the pocket of the seat in front of me, stare at other people, count the number of blinds on the window, or go and get hot chocolate.

In the beginning, what I enjoyed about these outings most was getting to listen to music and dressing up. It made me excited to have something to treat as a celebration. I know now when you begin following Jesus a lot of life becomes a celebration. It's awesome.

As I continued going to church with Rosie and her family, I started to enjoy even more aspects of Sunday: the people, parts to the message I could make out and understand, and prayer that resonated with me.

Although I still spent some Sundays more focused on doodling and hot chocolate, I wanted to keep going because I liked the way I felt afterward. Eventually, I started inviting myself to church even on the weekends I wasn't at Rosie's.

I'd think to myself, *Maybe if I continue pursuing this path, God will make me into someone like Rosie.* However, I started to second-guess that idea the weekend Janie, Rosie's mom, took us to a Christian conference for young girls.

I'll never forget feeling entirely out of place as I watched all of the girls my age singing and dancing to the songs being played on stage, not caring what anyone around them thought. I wanted to be one of the girls to sing and dance too, but I was afraid I'd be seen as nothing more than a big phony.

I don't remember too much of what was said that weekend, and I ignored the invitation Jesus was extending for me to come and follow Him because I was too busy telling myself I'd never measure up.

What Is a Christian and Who Is God?

Not long after our weekend away, Janie took me to pick out my first Bible, which allowed me to feel slightly more comfortable in church.

Although I still faced that "not enough" feeling, I wanted to know if I could actually start over like everyone had said I could. Shortly after receiving my Bible, I started going to youth group with Rosie to find out the answers to my long list of questions.

Are God and Jesus the same person?

Will I still make it to heaven even though I've cussed, done things with boys I'm not proud of, and have stolen from the store?

How do I keep myself from falling asleep when I'm praying before bed?

What am I supposed to say when I pray?

Do I pray to Jesus, God, or the Holy Spirit?

What if I can't remember the fourteen generations and the list of names in the book of Matthew and every other book in the Bible that starts with a long list of people?

How can I be a Christian if I can't even remember the basics?

I went to youth group, not for snacks or games, but because I saw it as another way to absorb information. I'd go every week and sit with my notebook open and pen in my hand. I needed to figure out what exactly Christians believed, and if it was something I was going to believe as well.

After the teaching, I'd retreat to a less-crowded table to reflect on all that had been said. I wanted to make sure I didn't miss anything.

My eagerness to learn soon became recognized by our youth pastor, and when he was done speaking, he would gently set his notes down on the table next to me as I scribbled something with a focused look and much determination.

The only thing I knew about God at this point was He loved me. He knew about my past and wanted a relationship with me regardless. Honestly, I think that's one of the most important things for us to know about God always.

I also knew as I continued hanging out with Rosie, there would be people (mainly other girls at school) who asked her if she was crazy, while criticizing me for suddenly claiming I was a changed woman.

There was a lot of fear stored up inside of me about how my decision to follow Jesus and continue being friends with Rosie would affect both her life and my own.

However, when I look back, I see even in my doubt and confusion, God continued to pursue me. Through people, events, and love, He created a path to lead me closer to Him.

I don't know what bumps lie in the middle of the path or how long the path even is, and I don't think Jesus expects me to know every answer. Just like His disciples, He wants me to know who *He* is, to follow *Him*, and to trust and do what *He* says along the way.

Such a simple concept, yet so hard for the majority of us to do. In the six years I've been following Jesus, there have been many times I've reached a spiritual low or insisted I knew the best route to get me where I wanted to go.

I did this all throughout my eating disorder, and today I find myself doing it in career choices and relationships.

Meeting My Maker

My "come to Jesus" moment—as many people call them— was at a second youth conference I went to in 2011 with my youth group called Acquire the Fire.

Although most testimonies sound alike and get shoved into the same category of when a person first meets Jesus, I think God speaks to each individual differently in those moments. In fact, I believe God is always speaking to us, inviting us to rest and take shelter in His refuge, yet it's in small moments when we are hit with the reality of His name and reminded we're not alone.

I once heard a pastor say, "We were meant to know our Maker, but sin has this separating effect." I'll never forget that.

There's a really popular Christian song that talks about failing a thousand times and still being given God's mercy, grace, light, and glory. This song was playing the night I came to know my Maker, and the lyrics left an imprint on my heart. Each word was a declaration, an end to my loneliness, a breath of fresh air, a place to rest my head. Comfort, freedom, joy.

The call for me that night was to trust in God more than I trusted my father on Earth to be there for me. I, along with several other individuals, was invited to come up and receive prayer if we resonated with being let down by our earthly fathers time and time again.

Because I still saw myself as an imposter, I tried to ignore the call. That is, until I began sweating and my heart was beating outside of my chest. I knew from being to so many church events thus far, this usually meant whatever was causing your heart to thud was a step you needed to take.

Before I knew it, I was surrendering myself to God for the first time.

For so long, I had been responsible for my well-being and unable to rely on every adult I was told I could trust. Having an absent father was not fun. It made me sad and it stung... It still stings. Yet, I didn't always have time to process my sadness because I was too busy being a parent to myself.

That night was the first time I began to process my sadness through worship, and it was the first time I felt my sadness was accepted. I was crying to release the tension and anger

I had stored up and crying because, in my darkness, I was beginning to see Light that shone brighter than any other—a sense of peace and a Father who kept His promises.

I don't remember everything from the week of ATF, but there are a couple of things I won't ever forget. First, I won't ever forget the wall torn down inside my heart, allowing me to receive grace the night Jesus spoke truth over me. I won't forget the comfort I felt and the chains broken with each uncontrollable tear shed.

Second, I won't forget the bus ride home where Rosie and I held each other, crying and laughing with love and excitement in our hearts. I still have yet to see one of my friends who doesn't know Jesus have their life transformed before my very eyes. But Rosie? She saw it all.

She saw me go from being timid and afraid of what other people thought to nudging my way past her as I walked to the front of the stage and sang at the top of my lungs to the God I spent a majority of my childhood not knowing.

She saw me go from being boy crazy to being bible crazy, from dwelling in my circumstances to being joyful in them.

By the end of the bus ride, I don't think we knew whose snot and tears were whose, but we didn't care because of the overwhelming, all-consuming love surrounding us.

We both saw through different lenses that night how far both trust and prayer will get you when you stop thinking about everything you can't do and start believing in everything God says He is going to do.

The Pressure to Be Perfect

The desire and attempt to be perfect has followed me my whole life and is one of the biggest reasons I feared following Jesus in the beginning. I was always thinking, *Who am I kidding?*

Thanks to the Enneagram and other personal development tools, I've come to understand both the helpful and harmful effects of my perfectionistic tendencies as a One. Riso labels Ones as Principled Teachers and expands on how necessary we find it to be right and to do right in the world:

> They want to put objective values into practice and to be unswayed by their passions, so that, as much as is humanly possible, they can do whatever is objectively right... They do not want to sacrifice their principles because to do so would corrupt their integrity, and by violating their integrity, they would ruin something essential, their capacity for goodness and virtue, sources of deep satisfaction to them.[26]

Even with the deep desire to be and do right, however, I still found it difficult to quit hanging out with my older friends after my big encounter with God. I found myself clinging to old ways because of the lingering voice telling me I wasn't ready. I faced an incessant worry that the life Rosie, her

---

26 Riso, *Personality Types*, 284-285.

family, and so many others were experiencing wasn't within my reach. My life was still so ugly, and I didn't know how it would smooth out.

It makes sense to me now why I would have felt that way. I think whenever you have some sort of transformative moment, especially with God, it conflicts with what is already known, expected, or deemed normal in a person's life. It's transformative because it brings forth transformation. Yet, to see this transformation in full takes time because following Jesus is a process.

The moment the transformation sparks is only the beginning. For me, much of the days after my encounter with God felt scary. To trust God *is* scary. I found myself slowly and cautiously dipping my toes into the waters of Christianity, but it took a long time to fully trust I wouldn't fall. There was a lot of "fake it until you make it" behavior happening, and there was even more doubt.

I don't belong here.
Who do I think I am?
This path is terrifying.
This path is long.
I have so much to learn.
I'm no different than I used to be.

On top of doubt, my monsters knew exactly how to tap into my perfectionism. They'd ask me, *If you can't do this thing perfect, why do it at all?*

One of the main reasons I fell victim to these false narratives was due to the common misconception of Christians being one of two things:

1. Flawless humans who have a perfect, cookie-cutter life.
2. Hypocritical and never matching their actions to their words.

The truth I've found is there are some hypocritical people out there. All of us can be hypocritical at times, saying one thing and doing another. It's in our nature to be imperfect, yet I think Christians especially become an easy target to throw the word "hypocritical" at because too often they get associated with the word "perfect" or "good."

When talking about someone you know, have you ever heard the phrase they *grew up in a Christian home*? Better yet, have you ever had someone say of another family they are *good, Christian people*?

This language gets thrown around all the time and is so funny to me. I think sometimes we forget growing up in a Christian home or calling ourselves a Christian doesn't make us "good."

It's no wonder why whenever a scandal happens in the church so many people are shocked and angry. These pieces of news give our world even more ammunition to throw at the church with words about how hypocritical its people are.

We get too caught up putting our trust in pastors and other thought leaders, rather than putting our trust in God. Often we forget Christians are still human, accustomed to human nature just like everyone else. Born into sin and influenced every day by the world we live in.

The only difference between a non-believer and believer in terms of "goodness" is they follow someone perfect and mighty in all His ways. We have been renewed by Jesus and given true Life by *His* good works, and it's important to remember it is God who is perfect—not Christians.

Are there Christians who think they are perfect? Yes. Pride is another condition of our nature, but so is lust, lying, and cheating. However, another difference between non-Christians and Christians is we are not alone in our humanness and have Jesus, a real person who walked this earth just as we do. He is a friend who can relate to us, and a brother who provides access to Yahweh, the Creator of all things.

This doesn't mean we are free from making mistakes, yet it does mean we won't ever be alone in our mistakes.

There will be days we fall, but it is in those weak places we have a helping hand to lift us, lead us to water, and carry the load of our wrongdoings.

If Christians were perfect, we wouldn't need Jesus, and let me tell you, I need Jesus every day, all the time, one hundred percent. And thank goodness I do because I've tried to be perfect over and over and it's hard, impossible, and exhausting!

The reason I'm sharing this is that I needed to hear it when I was deciding whether life with Jesus was for me.

I needed to know Christians are people, too—a mixed bag of goods just like everyone else—who are in process and doing the best they can.

The Best Day and Days to Come

The summer following my sophomore year of high school, I wanted to make my decision to follow Jesus public through the waters of baptism. The truth is I *was* set free from my past. When I accepted Jesus, I didn't just accept part of His story, but all of it, even the parts of it I didn't quite understand or had yet to learn.

There won't ever be a time when I'm all-knowing, without questions, and fully comfortable in my relationship with Jesus. That's why I need God, and that's why I have faith. It is Him who is all-knowing, all present, and all-powerful. In other words, He is omniscient, omnipresent, and omnipotent.

On August 12, 2016, I was baptized by my youth pastor. Rosie and her family were there, as well as a few of my friends, my dad, and his parents.

I imagine the way I felt that day is similar to the way people feel on their wedding day. After all the build-up and stress, of course. I was:

Happy.
Content.
Taken care of.
Loved.
Excited.

There are few moments in my life thus far when I have felt all of those feelings at once. Perhaps when I'm older, I will think differently, but at this stage, the day I came up from the waters of baptism was easily one of the best days of my life and a decision I won't ever regret.

It was loving people, summer camps, conferences, concerts, notes, and youth groups that got me to that very moment. And when I think back to all the church sermons I sat through, completely and utterly distracted, I smile at the compassion God had for me in His heart.

We all have gunk in our lives that often feels like a heavy load to carry, and the beauty is we don't have to carry our gunk alone.

I realize now it was never my responsibility to become like Rosie. I've always been meant to be Carly, and God is constantly showing me what she looks like when she isn't so worried about everyone else.

Do you feel pressure to be perfect?
Are the responsibilities you carry weighing you down?
When you look at yourself in the mirror, do you think of yourself as a fake?

You are not alone.

Whoever you are, wherever you are, there is an invitation for you to experience freedom and joy in your own life, too. You don't have to worry about spots filling up because there will always be a place for you at the table.

Take it from Jesus when he says the following:

> Come to me, all who labor and are heavy laden, and I
> will give you rest. Take my yoke upon you, and learn
> from me, for I am gentle and lowly in heart, and you
> will find rest for your souls. For my yoke is easy, and
> my burden is light.[27]

That's His invitation now and forever.

---

27 Matt. 11:28-30 (ESV).

PART 2

DISASTERS AND DISORDERS

CHAPTER 7

FINDING YOUR WORTH WHEN YOU FEEL UNWORTHY

———

"Real freedom means 'free at heart and free in mind.' You have to begin to realize that you are worthy and to remind yourself of this every day. You have to rebuild the positive levels of self-preservation that your self-esteem needs to heal."

—SHANTEL PATU[28]

There I was, sitting at the top of a hill on a random, dead-end country road wondering, *How did it come to this?*

The safe bubble I thought I could keep myself in dissipated and all I wanted was for God to *please tell me what to do.*

———

28 Shantel Patu, "Can Words Really Hurt Me?," *The Gottman Institute: A Research-Based Approach to Relationships*, May 29, 2019.

I wasn't a bad kid and my dad knew that, yet he'd use any small slip-up to take away gifts and belongings, one of them being my car. It must have given him a sense of control. After several unreasonable and unpredictable occasions of this happening, I decided I didn't want the car anymore, or the drama.

Earlier that afternoon, I was collecting all of my belongings from the vehicle when my dad arrived home.

He asked me what I was doing, and I explained to him the reasoning above.

My brother's car was parked on the road at the time since he was letting me borrow it for the week, and when my dad noticed this, he started to boil. I knew whatever argument was about to erupt wasn't going to be good and reminded myself to stay calm.

That's when he told me to get out of the car and leave the box I'd been filling up with my belongings.

When I reached for a couple more items, he again demanded I get out and told me he owned everything in the vehicle, including me. I knew he'd been drinking at this point and assumed the best thing for me to do was take my box of stuff and go to my room.

Only when I tried, he yanked the box from my hands, and when I went to pull back on the box, he pulled harder.

Moments later, I laid with my head down on the back seat, feet dangling out of the car, as I tried to grasp the reality of my father putting his hands on me for the first time. Pushing me with force and aggression, he walked away like it was something I deserved. My eyes began to flood with tears.

I had seen my dad time and time again let physicality be his method of establishing power, yet I never thought I would be the next victim to succumb to that sort of abuse.

In less than a minute, I was up on my feet and heading toward the garage where he stood with the box. Before I could say anything, he turned around and got as close to my face as he could to repeat the following with rage and anger, over and over:

"I'm the fucking boss, Carly. You are only sixteen."

Each word jolted a stress response within my body.

I reached for the box one last time, hopeful he had made his point and I could walk away from it all. Instead, I watched it crash against the garage door. Books unbound, photos absorbing the moisture of the concrete, jewelry tangled, and pencils slowly rolling down the driveway.

I gathered what I could in my arms, ran into my room, and locked the door. I prayed he would just leave me alone. The doorknob jiggled back and forth as I sat on my bed afraid of what would happen if I were to open it. The walls began to vibrate from the banging, and I remained frozen.

When I opened the door, he burst through and again stood directly over me. "Do you want to challenge me?" he asked.

I said nothing.

Again he asked, "Do you want to challenge me?"

I don't know what he thought I was challenging him about.

He continued, "Basically, Carly, you're not the fucking boss. I make the rules and if you choose not to follow them, there will be consequences. So, do you want to challenge me?"

I just looked at him, hurt and scared. When I didn't say anything the sixth or seventh time, he said, "That's right. You probably don't because I will win."

He then proceeded to lay out the details of what my day-to-day was going to look like from there on out. I would go to school and come home—that was it. I would walk to and from school, accepting no rides.

I was to have my brother come and pick up his car, and I wouldn't be driving it whatsoever. I wasn't allowed to play sports, and there would be a list of chores for me every day when I got home. No more phone, no more friends—this was the price I had to pay for trying to "challenge" my dad.

In a way, I already felt I had been beaten down by my father, not physically, but emotionally. The push wasn't what hurt me that day. It was the aggressive language, threatening, making me feel trapped, and letting me know what he thought of me when he chose to throw my belongings at the garage, scream into my crying face, and loudly declare *he* was the boss.

Not my dad nor my friend. Not someone I could trust or lean on. Not someone who was there to listen to me. No, he was the boss. *The fucking boss.*

When he retreated to the back porch that afternoon, Andrea arrived home from work and it was as if nothing ever happened. The smell of their cigarettes lingered through the hallway and made me sicker to my stomach than I already was. My tears transformed into intense focus as I tried to come up with a plan for how I might escape. I couldn't stay in that house another night and started packing the first items I could get my hands on.

Then, when no one was looking, I made my way out to my brother's car. Heart pounding and nausea in full force, I threw my bags in the back, got in the car, and started driving. I couldn't believe I'd left. I had deliberately gone against my father's word and gotten out successfully. However, I hadn't even made it three blocks before realizing I'd left my phone behind.

Shoot, shoot, shoot, shoot.

Pounding the steering wheel, I decided I had to go back.

I prayed when I arrived they would still be out smoking on the back porch. Closing the door as quietly as possible, I made my way up the drive and sighed in relief when I got to my bedroom seconds before he and Andrea came inside.

Only, now what? There was no way the escape plan was working *again*. I was going to have to be much more clever.

I went to the bathroom, washed my face, and combed my hair back into a ponytail. Then, I walked out to the kitchen and instinctively grabbed the Windex and paper towels.

"What are you doing?" my dad asked.

"Well, you said I had to give my brother his car back and part of the deal was I'd give it back clean."

That wasn't a lie. It was part of the deal.

He looked at me with skepticism but didn't question me further. Instead, he just watched as I walked out to the curb where the car was parked. As far as he knew, all my stuff was still in my room.

Pretending I didn't see him, I began wiping down the windows from the inside out. Once I saw him disappear from the corner of my eye, I waited three more minutes. Slowly and obsessively, I wiped each window with precision.

When he didn't reappear, I—as fast as I could—threw the Windex and paper towels into the passenger seat, started the engine, and stepped on the gas with all my might.

That's when I ended up on the dead-end road.

I didn't want to go to my mom's or my grandma's because I knew those would be the first places my dad went looking for me.

I didn't know where to go. Most of us have people in our lives who have continuously told us, "Hey, if you ever need anything, I'm here." Yet in a moment like this, I didn't feel capable of calling any of those people.

I needed my mom more than anything.

"Hey, sis."

Silence.

"Hello?"

Silence again.

"Carly?"

"Hey, Mom."

"Carly, where are you? Sweetie? Is everything alright?"

"No, it's really not."

Again, I lost control. Doing my best to talk through the tears, I told her what had happened.

You may be thinking, *It was just a push*. The truth is, it was *one too many* pushes, and I wasn't going to be defeated anymore.

I deserve love.

I deserve happiness.

I deserve to feel safe.

None of those things were present in my father's home.

I ended up meeting my mom and brother that afternoon, and they took me to the police station to retell the story of what happened.

Not surprisingly, the police weren't able to do anything. My dad had full custody, and there were no exterior bruises or marks to prove my story as true. So, I had two choices:

1. Go back to my dad's.
2. Stay the night at his parents' and return to his house the following day.

Two lousy choices if you ask me.

Between the time the officer heard my story and gave me my options, he responded to a call my dad made to the station reporting me as a runaway.

I still don't know the specific details of the conversation he had with my dad that day, but my guess is it went something like this:

I was being dramatic and overreacted.

I was sixteen and hated not being able to get my way.

I didn't like discipline.

It didn't help my dad knew and was friends with most of the policemen in the town I grew up in. Not only that, but Andrea was previously married to one.

It was like the police officer had changed personalities when he reentered the room. He had an assertive demeanor and went from being open to listening to my story and helping me get somewhere safe, to firm in his decision and unwilling to negotiate.

I couldn't believe it. Once again, I was outnumbered. Once again, it was his word over mine. Once again, my fear, pain, and sense of threat and danger did not matter.

My dad was right. He would win but not for long.

Begging for Someone to Please Just Listen

My brother stayed with me at my dad's parents' the night we left the police station, and first thing the next day, we headed to the Department of Human Services (DHS).

I had a sour taste in my mouth whenever someone brought up talking to DHS because I had already gone to them twice when I was younger.

If they didn't do anything about my living situation then, why would they do anything now? But I was desperate. *Maybe this will be the one time they take me seriously.*

Blue ribbons were hanging from trees and blowing in the wind outside, and the office walls were covered in educational posters highlighting April as Child Abuse Awareness Month.

"Can I help you?" the receptionist asked.

I wasn't sure where to start and began to pour everything out to the woman. I could tell she was rushed, and she could tell I had a lot to say, not just about the night before but about the last eight years.

Another woman soon came to get me and brought me back into a cold and windowless conference room with nothing but a phone.

Stay positive, Carly.

I waited in the bare room, stuck in my head with nothing to distract me but a blinking red light coming from the phone and an abandoned pencil.

The woman returned and apologized. They were just *so busy.* She placed a card down on the table with a number and told me someone on the other end of the line would certainly be able to hear my concerns and walk through the next steps.

Then the monsters began.

Stupid. Stupid. Stupid. Stupid.

Why did you come here?

You knew they weren't going to do anything.

I yelled at them to *stop*, to *please shut up.*

Maybe they can help. Maybe whoever is on the other side of the line does have a plan for me to follow. After all, it is Child Abuse Awareness Month.

I made it past the automated voice and spoke with a real person on the phone about what had happened, and what had been happening.

No, I wasn't injured or in immediate danger, but I was afraid of what would happen when I returned home. I didn't want to go back. I *couldn't* go back.

Her advice was to turn myself into a shelter service for youth who've experienced abuse, neglect, homelessness, or who have run away. I kept reiterating to her I had a family. I had so many family members who would gladly take me in, family who were healthy and able to care for me. I wasn't a troubled teen.

When I knew the conversation wouldn't ever reach the end I wanted it to, I hung up. I felt like my twelve-year-old self again. I had been here before, in this place of not being safe, but being safe *enough*. All I wanted was someone to *please just listen to me.*

I walked out as fast as I could, head down, nose runny, and cheeks red. Any more blue to flash in front of my eyes and I was certain I'd rip it down. The posters, the ribbons—it all felt foolish to me, like a hoax.

My brother didn't ask any questions. He didn't need an explanation. My body language said it all. We sat in the parked car, quiet.

"I'm sorry, Carly."

I told him to please take me to school. There wasn't time to be sad anymore. This was it. We did what we could, and it was time to return to reality, the reality that my dad did own me.

Accepting a Reality I Despised

By the time we reached the school, I had stuffed down all my leftover feelings to deal with later. It turned out there were more leftovers than I anticipated.

Before I knew it, my health teacher was pulling me out of class after sensing I wasn't myself. I've never been good at hiding my feelings.

Next, I was pulled into the Dean's office, then the principal's office, and lastly, the school counselor's office. So many people who cared, yet who simply didn't understand the controlling nature of my father.

All of their suggestions were fantastic alternatives I had thought and dreamt several times; however, to get such ideas past my dad would be impossible. My school decided to call

DHS to validate my request, saying they did not feel it was safe for me to return home either.

But there were no bruises, at least, none that were visible.

When the school day ended, my brother picked me up and we made our way back to our dad's.

We planned to have an adult conversation when we arrived, asking him to let me stay with another family member for a few days. The school counselor found this the best idea for the meantime. My brother would lead the conversation, and I would follow.

An adult conversation was the furthest thing from what we had that afternoon. Within minutes, my dad demanded my brother leave, threatening him to get off of his property because he wasn't a part of this. As he walked down the drive with big tears wallowed up inside his eyes, he never stopped looking back.

"I love you, Carly. Everything is going to be okay."

As soon as he drove away, I wanted to go lock myself in my room but unfortunately, that wasn't an option. Instead, my dad glared at me and made sure to point out how foolish I was for trying to run away.

"I have all the power in the world, Carly." He smiled.

I asked him, "Do you like seeing me like this, Dad? I'm not happy here. Why are you doing this to me?"

I told myself I would be strong, yet in that moment, all I felt was weak.

He continued on about how I would be under his control until I was eighteen and if I didn't want to follow his rules, my life was going to be one sad picture.

I left the conversation crying hysterically and went to my room scattered with belongings, the bed unmade, and my packed bags on the floor. Hours before, I thought it would be the last time I was there.

Curling up in a ball, I closed my eyes and tried to escape the present moment. My dad left for the bar and I stayed right where I was.

What am I supposed to do next? I'm out of options.

I had dealt with suicidal thoughts before, yet it wasn't until that afternoon when I felt tempted to put them into action. Maybe then, my dad might care. I wanted him to feel the emptiness he made me feel.

Moments later, there was a knock on the door.

It was Aunt Leanne. Well aware of what had happened and was still happening, she grabbed me and held me tight.

"Shh... I know."

"Shh..."

"You've got to calm down, Carly. I'm right here."

She said the reason she came was to talk to my dad about letting me go to Grandma and Grandpa's fiftieth wedding anniversary party that upcoming weekend. However, I truly believe my aunt had shown up that day because God sent her to stop me from harming myself. I was weak, and she came with strength.

She made the point my dad was going to keep saying hurtful things the more I continued to go against what he believed was right. But I had been following the rules. I had followed the rules so much he had to start searching for things to get mad about. It didn't work. Still, I trusted my aunt even if I didn't trust following the rules would get me out of there any sooner.

Two more years and I would be free. Until then, I needed to stay focused and be "good," doing whatever was necessary to win my dad's approval.

After my aunt left, I cleaned my room, unpacked and reorganized the mess I made when I left, took a shower, turned on some music, and did my homework. My dad got home, and I apologized for all that had happened.

I told him it was my fault. I was in the wrong, and I shouldn't have left. The hardest words I've ever forced myself to say, and the biggest lie I've ever told.

Less than a week later, things were back to "normal." My dad never stuck to his threats about taking away sports or my phone, and I was even given my car back (with terms and conditions, of course).

As long as I kept obeying his laws, I was able to slip under the radar just fine.

Your Struggle Is Real

I knew even though I wasn't happy living with my dad, I did have it better than most kids. But for too long I excused my safety and emotional health as ungratefulness because of the shame he pressed on me, telling me I should be thankful for the life I had.

I think many of us have been reminded how much better we have it. It's the classic line for parents to use at times like when you don't finish your dinner, and I'm not discarding any of that. However, I think it's important to remember the people better off than us, too.

Think about it. There are 7.6 billion people in our world, and there will always be someone better and worse off than us in whatever context you decide to use the phrase. So, we should be thankful for all we have, yet there also needs to be space for feelings of pain and insignificance to be dealt with.

We shouldn't have to dismiss our feelings or experience because of the obvious fact there are people in this world worse off than we are. Feelings aren't a competitive game. They are a reality that shape a person and feelings need to be expressed, especially in the younger years of someone's life.

When you shove emotions off to the side and don't create space for them, they seep out through the cracks of a person's being later on. I'm living proof of this, and maybe you are, too.

Were there times I overreacted when I was a kid and needed a reminder of how good I had it? Of course, I overreacted plenty of times and still do, forgetting the beauty in my life and replacing it with bitter thoughts. Still, there are necessary moments to aim for something higher and to grow into the kind person your friends and family need.

We get in this mindset of, "It could be worse," which only leads to a lack of personal responsibility. So often, I felt my dad using lines like this not to remind me of how beautiful my life was but as a scapegoat to cover up for his irresponsible behavior. To make me feel bad and to make himself feel better.

Even now, he clings to the rehearsed tape of all he's done for his kids, which makes it difficult to accept any gifts from him because I fear they will be used against me later.

I've never had security in the things he does for me because he always makes the point afterward to say, "I'm your dad, Carly. That's what a dad does," as if I've forgotten. I know how a dad is supposed to act. Thanks to him, I have a very clear image of how he's not meant to act, too.

Finding the Love You Deserve

If you've ever fallen victim to emotional abuse, I believe you. I've felt words be used as weapons, and I know how damaging certain behavior can be.

One Love, a foundation meant to educate young people on unhealthy relationships, came up with the below definition of emotional abuse:

> Emotional abuse is any abusive behavior that isn't physical, which may include verbal aggression, intimidation, manipulation, and humiliation, which unfolds as a pattern of behavior over time that aims to diminish another person's sense of identity, dignity and self-worth, which often results in anxiety, depression, suicidal thoughts or behaviors, and post-traumatic stress disorder (PTSD).[29]

It's important to remember emotional abuse is just as serious as any other type of abuse, and even if you don't have marks or bruises to prove your pain, the internal scars you carry have weight.

For years, I looked at myself as unlovable, so much so, I questioned if life was even worth living.

I wondered how anyone would ever see good in me if my own dad had trouble seeing it.

This is where I've found affirmations to be so powerful. Because even when you aren't getting the love and encouragement you need from the people around you, you can still give it to yourself.

---

29 "What Emotional Abuse Really Means," One Love Foundation, accessed August 30, 2020.

It might feel uncomfortable and even silly, but that's okay. I'm here with you.

These are the five "I am" affirmations that have helped me most. I want you to highlight them, write them down, put them on your mirror. Do whatever you need to do to let these words soak into your being so there is no more questioning your worth and seeking the approval and acceptance of others to feel like you are enough.

You can be that person, right here and right now.

So, repeat after me:

I am able to overcome whatever lies ahead because I am not alone.
I am fearfully and wonderfully made.[30]
I am loved and deserve kindness from myself and others.
I am not defined by the beauty standards placed on me by society.
I am stronger than my feelings and will choose joy, although I may not feel joy.

---

30 Ps 139:14 (ESV).

CHAPTER 8

STAY STEADFAST MY SOUL

"Your worst enemy cannot harm you as much as your own unguarded thoughts."

—BUDDHA

Shortly after the episode with my dad, I returned to a normal schedule and did everything I could to avoid being home. But normal only lasted about two weeks. After everything that happened between my dad and me, my mom decided to try filing custody papers again.

This was not the first time she had chosen to file, but the likelihood of her winning custody was greater than ever before.

The day my dad was served with custody papers, I got an ear full. He couldn't believe I had taken things to the extent I had, and he told me nobody would ever believe he pushed me down.

"You're going to regret this, Carly, and this is going to turn out badly for both you and your mom."

I tried to stay calm and not be intimidated by his threats.

While attempting to stay busy despite my circumstances, I reached for anything to bring more security to the instability I was facing. Two things I began devoting much of my attention to were my appearance and the food I ate.

I wanted to, as I always had, hide from the ugliness and stress at home. Most of all, I wanted to make myself smaller.

My friends didn't understand why I was so sensitive. I felt misunderstood by them and even myself. I'd fight back against my sadness because of the constant pressure I felt by my monsters to do more and to be more.

If I were to slow down, I'd have to confront the unpleasant reality of my life. The journal entry below is a prime example of how I felt daily:

May 15th, 2013
I stress and stress and stress about nothing. I have so much on my mind, yet I don't want to talk to anyone or do anything. I just feel like I'm letting everyone around me down and don't feel like I'm worth much.

I continued down a path of mild depression, masking my sadness and wearing a happy smile while falling apart inside. Then, something happened.

One of my teachers at the time happened to have a friend who was a lawyer in family law, and when I opened up to her about some of the things happening at home, she handed me a slip of paper with a name and number.

A few days later, I met with the family lawyer, Holly, and she agreed to represent me pro bono after hearing my story.

It was the first time I felt telling my story from beginning to end might lead to more than closed doors and tears, and it did.

There were still closed doors and there were still tears, only this time the doors were being shut on a chapter that should've ended long before, and the tears were tears of joy from finally being heard. Well, eventually. There is a bit more to the story.

Trying to Stay Hopeful

My dad reported me as a runaway a second time when I didn't come home after school and, instead, turned myself into the shelter recommended before by the woman on the phone at DHS. It turns out going there that day wasn't a complete waste of time.

Admitting myself to a shelter for youth was humbling and unlike anything I had ever experienced. All of my belongings were taken and locked in the basement when I arrived, and all I was allowed in my "room" were clothes, my book, my journal, and my hairbrush. There were lists of rules, hall monitors outside my door, and five other kids in much different situations than mine.

Although I constantly felt I didn't belong, I was willing to take the extremes necessary if it meant my case being taken more seriously by the courts.

When my time at the youth shelter was close to expiration, I met with Holly and we decided the best thing to do until we could get everything sorted out was to avoid school or contact with anyone. This involved staying with one of my cousins in a nearby town.

Everything about being considered a "runaway" worried me. My friends at school were being questioned, teachers and other people close to me wanted to know if I was safe, and being the Type A person I am, I didn't want to get behind on homework and hated missing school.

Being in hiding for what was supposed to be two days ended up lasting much longer. Our plans kept failing because my dad wouldn't agree to any type of solution my lawyer extended, and we weren't giving up until we had something in writing.

I just wanted to know where I'd be living so I could go back to being a kid. Or, at least attempting to be a kid. One of the days we went to the courthouse, I had a full-on breakdown because my biggest fear was we would run out of options and I'd be sent back to my dad's.

May 23rd, 2013
All I want is to be happy and to feel safe within the home I live.
It's not fair. Why me? I'm so angry at God. I keep praying while
in the back of my mind wondering, what's the use? Maybe I am
overreacting. Maybe I am just a "bratty little girl" like my dad
says I am. Is this my fault? I'm so tired and overly exhausted. I
just want everyone to be quiet and let me think for two seconds.

I've come to notice my way of dealing with depression is not the same as the ideal person. I'm so good at hiding any signs of sadness and hopelessness, even I do not know when I'm depressed.

Depression has come in waves throughout my life yet was the worst when trying to flee my father's home. I was dealing with suicidal thoughts regularly and felt numb to the world. My cousin who I was staying with for a brief time worked all day. I couldn't leave the house because of the risk of being seen and I remember sitting in her dark and quiet living room trying to make sense of everything happening.

One day when my cousin was at work, I raided her kitchen and ended up finding some ice cream in the freezer—Drumsticks. I vividly remember eating one of the ice cream cones while I stood by the counter, and afterward, I decided to eat another.

The creaminess and coldness against my tongue was a break from the heat of rising thoughts in my head. Until the ice cream was gone and the moment was over.

Then there was shame. It happened every time.

You're getting so fat.
Did you really need two?
No wonder you are alone.

Brené Brown defines shame as the "intensely painful feeling or experience of believing that we are flawed and therefore unworthy of love and belonging," and I felt that.[31] Not only in moments like the one above, but throughout my eating disorder, I tried to escape the shameful feelings and experiences I had.

I spent the remainder of my time hiding in eastern Oregon, six hours away from my dad. My mom's parents had decided to make the drive and take me with them to camp. We stayed at a family ranch and continued to wait for some sort of answer.

In the meantime, obsession over my body and food became more present.

May 25th, 2013
And we made it, safely! We are in Eastern Oregon at the ranch. Don't get me wrong... I'm so happy to be away but today has been bad. I started the day off wrong by eating donuts and then I ate way too much junk food. I've gained so much weight from not working out in over a week. I care too much what I look like and I'm so self-conscious of my weight. I hate it! I need to stop eating so much.

---

31   Brown, *The Gifts of Imperfection*, 39.

Many people would agree when I say it's the tough, defining moments in our lives that tempt our need for control, or rather the illusion of control, even more. This is true of my story, and you will continue to see moments like this unfold through the difficulty.

Part of this need came from doubt in God. To be new to faith during such a challenging and pivotal point brought its own trials. My built-up anger toward God kept me from pursuing Him, which in turn made Him feel farther away.

May 26th, 2014
Today was a good day. It has been too long. I saw both rain and thunder, along with sunshine. I stayed cooped up in the back of the truck canopy and came out once for lunch. Other than that, I just laid here. Read a book, got a lot of homework done, and talked to one of the closest people to me: Rosie. It was so good to laugh and finally be reunited with a friend. It made me feel somewhat normal.

I should start going to counseling. I think I might be depressed. And I'm not just being "defiant" or "overreacting" like dad always says. I honestly just think I need to talk to someone. I'm sad and this is a lot.

The most stable place I could have put my trust during this time was in God, and I'm now mature enough in my faith to know that. The events that unfolded weren't His fault, and I believe seeing me hurt caused Him hurt, too. As always, He was working in the background the whole time.

While staying at the ranch, I heard from my lawyer with news she had received something in writing from my dad agreeing to let me live with Rosie's family indefinitely. It was now safe for me to let people know where I was and to return to school. I was nervous. I was eager. I was in disbelief at the way things were going.

Our two-day plan had turned into two weeks, and although we now had an agreement, I feared what exactly that meant.

Would my dad send the police to get me tomorrow? If such a small exchange took two weeks, how long would the rest of this process take? There were a lot of unknowns up ahead, but I tried to ease my mind by focusing on the things I did know.

I knew I was about to be welcomed into a loving home. I knew I was going to finish out my sophomore year of high school. I knew I'd be seeing my friends and other people it had been so hard not communicating with while in hiding. Things were not set in stone, but they were pointing in a positive direction. For that, I was thankful.

Learning to Trust God in Uncertainty

If you haven't picked up on this yet, I'm an idealist who likes to think change is something that happens overnight. The world was moving quickly once I stepped back into my life of school, friends, and sports, and I wanted to forget about everything that happened with my dad. Shortly after being back in a steady routine, I believed such events were not relative, nor did they have space in what I was aiming to claim as a "normal" life.

I'm fine. I don't need to keep burdening those around me with the messiness of my life.

If I could just busy myself and do what I always did, if I could just pretend I hadn't been dealing with suicidal thoughts only a few days before. If I could just suppress, suppress, suppress, it would all go away—the bad thoughts, the bad feelings.

I'm normal now and so is my life.

June 21st, 2013
I got home last night and had a two-hour conversation with Janie in the car. She wanted to make sure I was doing okay living here. She said her hope for me while here is that I feel loved unconditionally. We talked about my dad and I told her I like staying here, but I'm scared when things are going good my dad is going to come at me unexpectedly and ruin everything. She told me to just be a kid because my dad would have to go through her and Paul first. Then she said whenever I get upset or start to worry, to have a Bible verse I can remind myself of. I think my verse will be Psalm 46:10: Be still and know that I am God.

Psalm 46:10 is still a verse I remind myself of when worry starts to bubble up or I find myself up against a crowd of anxious thoughts.

Goals and lists have always been something I turn to as sources of motivation and structure. However, I've learned trust is not a goal you can set a time frame for. To trust God will be a goal at the top of my list that I need help accomplishing the rest of my life. Yet when I'm still, and when I remember that He is God, doing so becomes that much easier.

It's truly breathtaking that God loves us so much, all He asks is for us to show up and give Him everything that's wearing us down; to hand all the gunk of our lives over, and in return, be set free.

Being Given a Choice

I lived with Rosie and her family throughout the summer and for the beginning weeks of my junior year of high school. And although I counted it as a blessing and enjoyed getting to pretend I was a kid with a perfect family and home, I couldn't forget about the mess with lawyers and court hearings that still had yet to be cleaned up.

Again I thought, *What if after all of this, I'm sent back to my dad's?*

I wanted a permanent place to call home and still feared I wouldn't ever have that. Bad dreams and monsters corroded my mind as I tried to sort through a mountain of questions and feelings.

July 28, 2013
I don't know what to do. I'm stuck. I'm depressed. I don't want to be around anyone and everything is making me upset. I feel sick to my stomach. I feel like somebody's watching me everywhere I go. All I wanted to do was come to grandma's, not talk to anyone, and curl up in a ball. I have a million things to do

this week that I don't want to do. I wonder if this is what life feels like when you're older. What if all I want is to be alone? I keep shutting people out. I don't know what I want. This is all too much, and I don't want anyone to get hurt. I feel so alone. I pray and still nothing. The sun is shining but I feel no warmth. I miss my dad, but I can't stand him at the same time. I talked to grandpa a little tonight. He was out in the shop doodling on some paper to try and distract himself from the pain in his legs. He told me how his mom kept a diary until the day she died and said he thought it was smart of me to keep one too. She used to pull it out and use it as guidance, I guess. I hope I can do the same.

My mom's parents' home has always been a safe place for me, and as Holly and I juggled options involving emancipation, I secretly wished to live there.

I knew this would hurt my mom, but the chances of me living with her were scarce. Not only that, but I was tired of feeling like a pawn in between her and my father.

When we were finally given a date to have the court hearing with my parents and both sets of grandparents, I got to confidently tell *my story* in front of a judge... something I had waited to do for nearly eight years.

And the outcome? My grandparents were granted guardianship over me. I got to choose. *I had won* and life was permanently going to change; such a foreign reality I couldn't wrap my head around.

The Purpose in My Struggle

I think back to these events, and there's a particular memory that sticks with me; the day Holly encouraged me to write out all that unfolded during this time. She said, "Who knows, maybe one day you will be able to get a book published."

Until then, I hadn't ever thought of writing a book. Then, a few years later, God told me I would indeed write a book. What about? I had no idea.

When I started writing *Good Enough*, I thought I was supposed to tell a story about my family and moving out of my father's home to help those in similar situations.

What I came to find out, however, is that this is only the beginning of my story. This is a small piece to a big puzzle.

So, Holly was right. I did get much of my recorded memories published, plus more. And my grandpa was right when he said keeping a journal was a smart idea. I've been able to, like his mother, look back at the entries for guidance... over and over.

If you're reading this, chances are, you're one of the very specific people God destined me to write this story for; someone who in the lowest of lows, has found themselves up against a wall of self-hatred; someone who has at some point, let circumstances take over and diminish every ounce of self-worth; a person who has felt amplified insecurity and overwhelming shame and guilt.

Maybe your particular struggle was the tipping point into an eating disorder, or maybe you just haven't seen yourself quite the same ever since.

It could be because you never healed you're trying to compensate by perfecting things around you, including your body. Or maybe food is the only thing bringing you comfort, and you're showing on the outside what you're feeling on the inside.

Maybe you're facing a combination of the above or something entirely different.

Regardless, I'm here for you.

I mentioned in the introduction I recently lost my friend, Kyle, to suicide. Less than a month before making the decision to end his life, he asked me this:

> Does that voice deep within still scratch at ya? I've always wondered... 'cause no matter what I do, there's still a voice deep down, telling me I'm worth nothing and will never amount to anything. I've always wondered, have you ever been able to conquer and defeat this voice? 'Cause it's getting the best of me right now.

My answer to him was, of course, yes. My monsters don't have nearly the same grip on me as they did before, which is why I wrote this book. I want you to be free from the voice or voices you face telling you you're not enough.

I am in agony knowing Kyle never had the chance to read *Good Enough* while on Earth, and I hurt so bad knowing he couldn't get his monsters to stop scratching.

After learning about his death, I questioned if finishing this book was even worth it. I was angry and confused and sad.

But isn't that what the enemy wants? To keep us from doing the things meant to lift people up out of darkness and into light? To bring upon us the most tragic thing right before a beautiful thing unfolds? To consume us with doubt?

I like to think of monsters as small seeds Satan plants. They're his helpers but don't forget who your help is. You have God on your side, and He's stronger than both. He takes evil and makes good; stone suddenly transforms into gold.

Kyle, I'm sure, sees this now even if he didn't feel it then. I hope you, my friend, know how valuable your life is even if the monsters in your head seem impossible to escape. Hold on tight. Don't let go. Stay steadfast.

CHAPTER 9

NOT SICK, BUT HUMAN

———

A friend once told me,

"I can see how being told you're beautiful can seem empty and shallow when inside, you know things aren't right. That feeling of being hollow is the worst. And it was easy for me to assume from the outside that, 'Carly should just snap it together! She's got it all... the look, the smile, the smarts, the tan, the effortless dress.' It was silly of me to be so naive. I wish I could have been a better friend to you. Your anxiety killed me."

Before I start this chapter, I want to thank you for hanging on this long. I hope at this point you've learned a thing or two. Maybe I've entertained you or helped you process some of your personality, an event, or feeling in your own life. Regardless, I want to say thank you.

I do also want to warn you I'm about to go into some serious details involving my battle with anorexia, bulimia, and exercise addiction. These are details I've wanted to share with you all along, but they first deserved some context.

I'm sure in the chapters before this you've started to notice for yourself how multidimensional eating disorders truly are. The relationships we carry, the events we experience, the insecurity and inner tension we feel—it is all connected to many of the outcomes we encounter in our lives—and every relationship, experience, and feeling matters.

The next portion of this book is going to be vulnerable as I share with you an addiction that shaped me tremendously.

As we continue, try to remember this is *my* story. If you or someone you know has battled an eating disorder, please do not make assumptions and compare my experiences to the one you know.

Eating disorders are complex, and there is no one cause, explanation, or cure.

Lastly, I'm not a professional, nor am I licensed to give any type of medical advice, diagnosis, or treatment. I am simply sharing my experience and what I've learned through my own eating disorder and recovery in hopes that it encourages those who are struggling to get the help they need.

If you are one of those people, know that *it is okay*. You are not alone in the battle, you will see it through, and this demon does not get to control you the rest of your life.

You don't have to apologize.

Be gentle with yourself.

You are not sick; you are human.

Mask After Mask After Mask

I've always struggled with body image. I'm a tall lady, and it wasn't until late high school when the boys in my grade finally started to sprout up and make me feel like less of a giant. For the majority of my upbringing, I was the one, and sometimes only, girl in the back of group pictures.

Everywhere I went, people would make it known, *Wow, you're a tall girl,* as if I didn't already know. So many comments I just stopped replying to.

You must play sports.

Your mom and dad must be tall.

Look at those legs!

It must be hard to find jeans.

I got used to ignoring comments made by others, yet what I couldn't ignore was the comparison plague that followed and consumed me once I hit eighth grade.

Many of my friends were stick thin and not nearly as tall. They had name brand clothes to fit them perfectly, their jeans were long enough to cuff, and they could wear tight shirts without worrying about their hips bulging out.

Their dresses and shorts were *always* school appropriate. They could run fast. Their selection of boys was much larger. Put simply, being short and skinny was better in my eyes.

I, on the other hand, wasn't stick-thin anymore. I didn't have name brand clothes to fit me perfectly. My jeans were rarely long enough, and I always wished I could cuff them because it was a major trend.

Tight shirts were off-limits because I thought I was fat when really I was just given hips I had yet to grow into at an early age. My dresses and shorts were never long enough for school, and even when they were, they still looked short because of my long legs. I couldn't run fast. My selection of boys was scarce. Put simply, being me—tall, uncoordinated, not yet fully grown and insecure—wasn't okay.

Another reason I liked hanging out with older girls when I was younger is that they had bodies more similar to mine.

Mary and Chay didn't have a ton of name brand clothes. Mary did have a lot of clothes yet wasn't afraid to wear generic brands. And the name brand clothes she did have, she had to work for. I remember one weekend we went to the mall to shop, and she taught me how to steal from Hollister in the fitting room.

I was so afraid and thought for sure we would get caught, yet the thought of wearing a t-shirt with a maroon bird and the words Hollister CO. printed across my chest was enticing enough to take part. When I went to school the next week and people ever so kindly told me I had a hole in my shirt, I laughed it off and pretended I didn't notice.

When I stopped hanging out with Mary and Chay, I felt different, and not in a good way. Parts of my body I was once insecure about, I started to obsess over, imagining and perceiving my normal body as deformed.

I started to wear lies as my new wardrobe and shame as my accessory.

You are flawed.
You are defective.
You are unloved.
You are nothing without makeup.
You are nothing without your hair done.
Everything others do, you must do better.
You must prove yourself lovable.
Selfie after selfie after selfie.
Mask after mask after mask.

I was afraid to walk the world uncovered as a young girl. Even when I wore my mask, bad things happened.

Once, I was invited to a birthday party with some of the most popular girls in school, the same ones who were mean to me when I was younger. When invited, I was told it wasn't an overnight party. We'd be shopping at the mall (something I never got to do) and eating at a fancy restaurant afterward, which at the time was Olive Garden.

I pretended such activities were anything but foreign, yet I was dying from excitement and hoped the day wouldn't ever end.

When we arrived back in our hometown, I was the first to get dropped off, and the next week at school one of my real friends let me know all of the girls had a sleepover after taking me home that day. I was hurt. More than anything, I was glad I didn't take my mask off.

I wondered how those girls would have treated me and what they would have done had I shown them a deeper layer. Events like this only validated my hiding, distrust, and fear.

The Comparison Plague

My whole life, I've been complimented and noticed a lot for my looks. Some attention, sweet and innocent. Other attention, unwanted and disrespectful. I say this not to sound conceited, but to say for most of my life I wasn't able to properly receive compliments because I simply did not believe them.

I knew how much work went into producing such an image each day. I spent hours standing in front of the mirror, analyzing and judging. Picking out everything that could be better and then trying to improve it. I'd wake up at five in the morning to do my makeup and would spend an hour before bed (sometimes more) choosing an outfit for the following day.

When given a compliment, all I could think was *If only they knew the truth, they wouldn't love me.*

Although I was unable to receive compliments, the attention—both positive and negative—was enough incentive for me to continue wearing my mask. It was safer that way.

I fed off attention so much that on days I didn't receive any compliments after dedicating so much time to my appearance, I'd take a photo or parade through public spaces to let it be known how "put together" I was. To undress and prepare for the next day of orders, I first needed validation.

If what I was seeking was left undiscovered, the false narratives I lived by got louder, and the demands placed on myself higher. It seemed I was able to recognize beauty in every other human being around me except for myself.

I didn't believe compliments given to me because I was too busy obsessing not only over the looks of others but over every small detail in the lives of those around me. Who were their friends and their family? What were the school activities they did and the sports they played? How did they perform in class, how did teachers treat them, and what were the grades they got?

It's the classic comparison plague we're all too familiar with. Only, my envy toward others went much deeper.

During eighth grade, I had an ovarian cyst twisting around my left ovary and fallopian tube, cutting off the blood flow. The doctors said the cyst was the size of a small cantaloupe, and I could have easily been mistaken as three months pregnant.

When I got out of the hospital, I had friends tell me, "We had no idea you were growing a cyst in your stomach! We just thought you were gaining weight." Such simple words meant no harm yet influenced much of how I viewed myself.

I'd notice a flaw and rather than shaking off my insecurity and moving on, I'd ruminate on it, thinking, *If they didn't say anything before when they noticed me gaining weight, why would they say anything now?*

I couldn't move on from my insecurities because I felt everyone else saw them, too.

Going back to my relationship with Rosie, I can honestly say she was the best and most pure gift to be given to me at a time when I lacked confidence and had difficulty seeing my potential. Yet, even with all of the wonderful things to come from our relationship that blossomed in seventh grade, comparison lingered.

When I was with her, I felt stuck in her shadow. She was tiny, funny, and popular. *Does she even realize how lucky she is?*

Rosie had a family who loved and prioritized her, parents who asked how her day was and genuinely wanted to listen when she answered. She had a mom who packed her lunch, and a dad who called her "sis." Parents who set the example of a healthy marriage and were always available to wrestle big questions.

She was good at school and didn't have to try. Everyone loved her. She could have people over without stress because she had a beautiful home that was clean and full of nice belongings.

I'd get upset it took her five minutes to pick out an outfit, when it took me thirty. I'd wonder why I didn't have the self-control to not eat everything on my plate, yet she could eat just as much—or more—and still have a perfect body.

I'd feel this way with other girls, too, but with Rosie, it was the worst because we spent so much time together. She was a constant reminder of what I didn't have, always wanted, and felt I would never get.

In her book 13 *Things Mentally Strong Women Don't Do*, Amy Morin talks about the damage comparison can have on your friendships. She says, "It's impossible to enjoy your friend's company when all you can think about is the fact that she's more fortunate or more attractive than you are."[32]

I felt this in my relationship with Rosie. Still, my envy never stopped her from filling me up with encouragement and complimenting the things about me I hated or failed to notice. She let me wear and borrow her clothes, even though I'd often stretch them out. She comforted me when I would cry and vent about things at home, and she gracefully let me claim her family as my own.

Even though I felt lost in Rosie's shadow, I realize she probably felt lost in my shadow, too. We'd often refer to each other as sisters, and like all siblings, there was a bit of envy on both ends that crept in. I know this to be true because when we sat down and talked for the first time in four years, we were both confronted with some hard truths of how each of us felt when we were younger.

---

32   Amy Morin, *13 Things Mentally Strong Women Don't Do: Own Your Power, Channel Your Confidence, and Find Your Authentic Voice for a Life of Meaning and Joy,* (New York: William Morrow, 2018), 27.

It was near the end of college, soon after Rosie had gotten married, and she invited me over one weekend when I was in town. We sat at her kitchen table for hours getting to know the people we had become while picking up the pieces of what had broken between us years earlier.

I always thought I would be one of the women to stand by Rosie's side when she said, "I do," but instead, I was one of the guests in the audience regretful of the friend I let go. She had regrets too. She apologized for not being there for me more during my eating disorder and asked me, "How could I have been a better friend to you when you were struggling?"

Sitting here now, I wouldn't have asked for anything more from Rosie because through this process I've realized it's me who should start asking that question. In middle school and high school, however, it's hard to see how anyone else is feeling. I, at least, was blind to how my actions were affecting others and sometimes still fail to acknowledge the feelings of those around me.

What I've noticed is this:
In elementary school, I was confused and felt alone.
In middle school, I felt I had to do everything on my own.
In high school, I took and took and took because I lacked the capacity to give.

But I want to start asking the friends in my life now, *How can I be a better friend to you in your struggle?* Now that I am healthy and able, *How can I love you?*

Learning To Be You

It wasn't until a couple of years into my recovery I was finally able to look at myself without judgment. I put together a no-makeup challenge with a group of women for two weeks, and for the first time, I walked the world uncovered. I did the very thing that scared me. Sometimes, chasing your fears is what it's all about.

What I started to notice during those two weeks is this: people still love me when I'm not wearing my mask. Granted, our masks often go deeper than a layer of makeup, yet small steps make for great strides. We can't let the negative experiences from our past dictate how we walk in the present.

Little by little, I've been able to uncover the Carly that God created with intent and purpose, the same intent and purpose He created you with. I've found a whole new side to myself, a silly one where I'm not so serious and make bad jokes only I think are funny.

Comparison still tiptoes in at times, and when it does, I acknowledge its presence before kindly letting it go. I remember that although the person I carry envy toward in that moment seems to have it all and be perfectly put together, we all carry our own set of insecurities.

I start to think about all God's done in their lives, while reminding myself of all He's done in mine, too.

Your timeline, circumstances, blessings, and role in this world will never match up with anyone else's, and you will forever share inward and outward differences with those around you. For this reason, comparison is inevitable.

But think about when you're older, with gray hair, near the end of your life. Looking back, I'll bet you never wish to have been someone else.

If anything, you'll wish you would have been you, the true you.

CHAPTER 10

THE ROOTS OF MY DISORDER

"Every relationship in your life is an overflow of the relationship you have to who you are."

—SARAHJANE CASE[33]

My access to food when I was younger was neither limited nor abundant. Rather, it was inconsistent.

When my mom was around, I associated food with feelings of joy and comfort because of the love she expressed through her cooking and giving. One example is when she'd pack my lunches before school.

I don't remember what exactly my lunch consisted of, but I do remember always having a note to look forward to once

---

33 Sarajane Case, "Enneagram and Relationships," July 2, 2020, in *Enneagram & Coffee*, produced by Sarajane Case, podcast, MP3 audio, 45:00.

lunchtime came. Even if I didn't see one right away, I'd be opening my sandwich container and, sure enough, would find it laying gracefully on top of my sandwich.

After my dad got full custody, sack lunches were no longer regular. Instead, I got switched to hot lunches like pizza, chicken nuggets, chocolate milk, and the cheap cheese they put on hoagie rolls, which looks and tastes like plastic.

Don't get me wrong, eating school breakfast and lunch wasn't horrible. I'm thankful both kept me from being hungry, and although I would have preferred Mom's lunches, I look back and laugh at some of the memories I have of cafeteria food. Does anyone else remember using napkins to dab grease off the soggy cafeteria pizza?

I will say, I was often jealous of those around me who didn't have to eat hot lunch. It hurt to see other kids opening notes up from *their* parents. Sitting down at the table with my lunch tray often caused me shame because I felt like everyone had noticed and felt the shift from sack lunches to hot lunches as drastically as I had.

My dad didn't keep the house stocked with groceries. Most of the time you were guaranteed to find the cupboards and fridge one of three ways:

1. Empty of food but full of booze.
2. Full of only necessities like rice, flour, bread, and milk.
3. Full of Top Ramen, stale cereal, lunchmeat, and canned goods.

Without my mom around, food wasn't the enjoyable experience it was before. It was just an experience, sometimes one of sadness, unpredictability, and stress. Other times, it was an adventure. Aside from my normal school meals, I never knew what I'd get.

Some days I'd get home from school and have no problem finding a snack. Other days, we'd be out of everything, and I just wouldn't eat. Even with the necessities, I didn't know how to make most things.

Weekdays were better than weekends because my dad normally only stopped at the bar for a couple of drinks before coming home to make dinner. On the nights he had darts (yes, he is a part of a dart league), I'd walk down to the bar or pizza parlor he was playing at, and he'd make sure I got some food.

The weekends, on the other hand, were more unpredictable because they called for later nights at the bar. If it was convenient for him, he might bring takeout home or have something planned, yet more often than not, the response I'd get after asking what's for dinner was, "There's plenty of food in the house." If I'd argue and say otherwise, he'd tell me he would bring me home something from the bar. When? I didn't know.

Inconsistent.

If my dad felt like cooking, he could cook and would cook well. He makes the best guacamole, burritos, steaks, and potatoes. Still, the act of eating was not enjoyable. We never sat around the table as a family, and after the divorce, I got used to him dishing up his plate and sitting in front of the TV in the other room.

Meanwhile, I'd sit either at the bar or table by myself.

I couldn't be trusted to not make a mess. If for some odd reason he was feeling spontaneous and did let me eat in the living room, I still couldn't enjoy the food or act of eating because I feared what would happen if I did make a mess. If I didn't like the food put in front of me, that was even worse.

Finding the courage to tell my dad I was full or didn't like something would stress me out too much to focus on the television.

At least when mom was around, she would calm me through each harsh demand from my dad to, "Eat your food!"

She'd tell me to, "Just eat three more bites, honey," or, "At least just try it, okay?"

But more than once, I remember my dad telling me things like:

"If you can't finish what's on your plate, you're going to bed."

"I'm done with you wasting food and being so damn picky, Carly."

"You're not getting down from that stool until you finish your dinner."

"I don't care if you don't like it. Eat it now."

"Aww, Carlos doesn't like what we are having? Too damn bad."

He'd snap at me every few minutes to finish eating my food because to waste food was unacceptable. Some nights my mom would win the battle and slip me a peanut butter and jelly, but most nights, it was my dad who proved his point.

I think back to the frustration I caused him by not eating my food when I was younger, and I also look back to all the times he decided what was for dinner. Never once did he ask me, "What do you want to eat, Carly?" Maybe then I would have eaten my food.

But that's not the way things were, and I can't help but think these patterns contributed to my relationship with food as I got older.

When I started playing basketball again in seventh grade, I'd be out to eat with my team after a tournament and someone would make the comment, "Jeez. You can eat so much and you're still so skinny!"

What people didn't realize is the reason I could eat so much around others is because I didn't eat much any other time.

As we started traveling to other cities for games and tournaments, I began to notice how rare it was for my family to eat out at restaurants. We'd be in the car and one of my teammates would point to a restaurant I had never heard of and rave about how good it was. When they found out I hadn't ever been there, they'd make all kinds of noise and say something to the extent of, *That's crazy.*

Whenever I did find myself in one of these talked-up places, I'd be overwhelmed by choices and people telling me, *You have to try the fries,* or, *The chicken is to die for.*

Most times I was the only kid without parents at our basketball tournaments, and although my dad would do his best to make sure he sent money with me, he often underestimated how much it costs to feed a kid at restaurants for a weekend. On multiple occasions, I'd have other parents tell me to, "Get whatever you want. We will take care of it!"

Whatever I want?

This kind of freedom was something I hadn't ever experienced. I'd get my food, and maybe a milkshake. I'd eat everything in front of me in no time and then I'd look around to see if any of my friends were done eating so I could finish their leftovers.

I'd eat, and eat, and eat. Eating so quickly and never having it register I was full until after leaving the restaurant, I would feel sick from all of the food I ingested. I started to become greedy with my food, despising those who would ask for bites of whatever I was having.

I ate fast because I feared food being taken away from me and didn't know when an opportunity to have choice over what I ate would come again. I took from the plates of others because I had been taught it was a cardinal sin to waste food.

I'd think, *If it's bad to waste food I don't like, wasting food I do like must be even worse.* So, I'd take on the responsibility of making sure it was all accounted for, even if it meant a bloated belly and poor night of sleep.

The amount of food I could eat soon became a badge of honor, and this behavior carried on into high school. At times my friends would use me as their portable trash can, disposing of anything they didn't want while assured I would take care of their scraps.

It reached a point where—even if I wasn't hungry—I'd still eat large quantities of food simply because someone challenged me to.

I couldn't properly gauge when I was hungry or full because I had been given so many regulations from my father when it came to eating. How I felt was never considered. My likes, my dislikes, my preferences—none of it mattered. I ate what sounded good to my dad, what he felt like having, what he liked, when he was hungry.

If I suggested something different, I was ridiculed. This happened with other situations not involving food too.

In her book *Eating in the Light of the Moon*, Anita Johnston expresses how women struggling with disordered eating were, as children, able to sense discrepancies in reality when those around them had varied descriptions and opinions of right from wrong. She writes:

When this young girl spoke truth or brought to light that things were not as they seemed, her truth was not well received. Instead, her statements were either ignored or met with fear and hostility from family members or authority figures... This put the young girl in a very uncomfortable position. In order to survive, she had to find a way to conceal who she really was, to diminish this ability to see the invisible, to quiet the voice inside of her that spoke the truth... She did this by accepting others' perceptions of reality and rejecting her own... She then continues through life with the assumption that there is something very wrong with her... She must recognize her bright, intuitive nature for the gift that it is even though others' discomfort with it has brought upon her some struggles and emotional wounding. She must begin to assert, both to herself and the world around her, that she is not defective.[34]

You see, intuition was a foreign concept as I got older because I was so used to rejecting my thoughts, feelings, and body's needs.

Food as a Metaphor

Overeating was never an issue at home, but when I did make snacks after school, I'd turn on the television instantly. TV, music, and podcasts have all been used as attempts to close the door on my monsters. When I was younger, they helped shut out the voice telling me I was unloved and forgotten,

---

34 Anita Johnston, *Eating in the Light of the Moon: How Women Can Transform Their Relationships with Food through Metaphors & Storytelling* (Carlsbad: Gurze, 1996), 17-18.

and as I got older, they shut out the voice of judgment telling how much I should and shouldn't eat.

With all of these things, my monsters only disappeared for so long before finding a way to tell me I wasn't doing enough. *You're lazy, lethargic, and pathetic.*

When I'd eat with my basketball team or Rosie's family, my monsters kept quiet and it was rare I felt guilt or shame over the food I ate.

I think most of the adults around me knew enough about my home life to know I wasn't eating as much as I should. So, they encouraged me to grab seconds and to have dessert, too. Only when my body started to mature did my monsters start to widen their vocabulary.

There is something wrong with you.
Your body doesn't look like hers, or hers, or any of theirs.
Your body is different.

Eating soon became my coping mechanism when I was stressed or scared. I had a lot of feelings I didn't know how to deal with or process, so I sought to protect myself by stuffing myself. All this did was create even deeper self-hatred, a desire to detach from my body—the very creature I deemed evil—and more determination to be in control of its gluttonous desires.

Do you see how food is only a metaphor for deeper lies one carries? It is true eating disorders are addictions, yet it's the behaviors that are addicting, not the food.

Johnston argues those with eating disorders will never satisfy their needs through food because it's their heart and spirit that needs to be filled. She explains it this way:

> Someone who is addicted to eating is actually starving on an emotional and spiritual level. Her longing for food is a longing for emotional and spiritual nourishment. It is often a longing for the ideal mother, the archaeal Good Mother who nourishes us, soothes us, loves us, and accepts us just the way we are. Frequently, this is the "something" she searches for as she stands in front of the fridge. This is really what she is in pursuit of when she sets out for the grocery store. No matter how much ice cream she eats, how many cookies she consumes or muffins she devours, she cannot fulfill this longing because she is filling her stomach, not her heart, not her spirit.[35]

I can't tell you how many times I faithfully returned to my eating disorder behaviors with trust they would provide escape. Then, before I knew it, I'd be ruminating on a food experience, torturing myself with regret, and listening to the monsters telling me I must work for or get rid of the food.

After events like this, I'd rely solely on self-control to reel me back into what was "good" by only eating healthy foods and restricting my caloric intake.

---

35   Johnston, *Eating in the Light of the Moon*, 34.

Tomorrow I will do better.
I won't eat until lunch.
I'll swim a bunch at the lake, and it won't matter.

I wanted to move on from these thoughts but couldn't get away from my morphed ideas of beauty.

The Lies Society Tells You

Growing up, it seemed fat-shaming was more present than any other table conversation in my friend and family circles. Speaking of people who lived in fat bodies as inhuman, disgusting creatures who cared nothing of themselves and sat on the couch drinking soda and eating cake all day.

In public spaces, my dad has asked questions like, "Have you noticed it doesn't matter what the weather is like—fat people are always wearing shorts?" He's also found it humorous to make jokes about how I need to watch my weight as I'm ordering my food.

My dad knows little to nothing about my fight with disordered eating, and I don't think he cares to. Like most people, he thinks it's more about an image than it is a mental illness, a way to get attention and stay skinny.

All it takes is going out to dinner with a group of people, being inside a fitting room with friends, eavesdropping on conversations nearby in a clothing store, turning on the TV, reading a magazine, looking at food packages, or doing a workout led by a fit instructor for us to find ourselves in the torment of diet culture.

All around us, there are messages that not only correlate thinness with beauty but with identity, self-worth, belonging, and "goodness."

At dinner, people say things like:

Well, this pizza is going to go straight to my hips...

I'm actually not eating that right now but thank you. I started a new diet this week. Hopefully, I'll finally see some results from this one.

Oh, I should probably get the salad. I have a wedding coming up and need to lose a few pounds, so I'm not eating carbs.

Vegetables are carbs, people!

In the fitting room, we hear:

I need to lose weight. I cannot believe I'm a size ten.

I hate my thighs.

I wish I could wear tank tops more. My arms are so flabby!

Ugh... you are so tiny! It's not fair. Everything looks good on you.

On the TV, there are weight loss ads, plastic surgery promotions, fat jokes, comments on dieting, crazy extremes people put themselves through to lose weight, the perfect pill to suppress your appetite (because we've been trained to believe that having an appetite is a disgusting burden we shouldn't dare listen to), and much more.

Oh, and should I dare mention the flood of skinny main characters across television?

In magazines, you find before and after photos designed in a way that makes the person always look so much more depressed in the before photo than the after one. It's almost like you can't be happy and live inside a fat body.

We read success stories of celebrities and how they've accomplished such praiseworthy weight loss and are just *so healthy.*

On the other hand, we read shame stories of celebrities, how they have gained so much weight and have completely let themselves go. Never mind if the weight is baby weight—*lose it, quick, before it's too late!*

During workouts led by an instructor, they'll tell you, *The pain of exercise is far less than the pain of regret!*

All of these words, ideas, and diets are preached, sold, and used in ways that directly assume our worth to be dependent on our weight and image. Beliefs food can't be enjoyed, and beliefs one cannot celebrate with friends until they look a certain way.

Encouragements to deprive and restrict your body, completely denying any sort of mind-body connection. Fear of food and fear of shame make people believe if they eat a certain way or carry fat, they will be both talked and joked about.

This mindset is what initially propelled me into believing the food I ate must be worked for.

The Beginning to a Long Body Dysmorphia Journey

During the volleyball season of my freshman year of high school, I'd run a mile through my neighborhood after practice if I felt I didn't get enough of a sweat in.

It got to the point where running or doing a Jillian Michaels "Six Week Six Pack" workout video after practice wasn't a choice anymore. It was a requirement before I could eat dinner and before I could relax.

Working out after practice wasn't a hard mountain to climb and was just another way to occupy my mind from dealing with everything at home.

Such exercise only felt forced when my monsters relentlessly chimed in about how I had failed that day if I didn't carve out the extra time. In my mind, I had no reason to be upset with the way I looked if I wasn't doing anything to change it.

One day, I bought cellulite cream after reading an article on Google about how to get rid of those hideous dimples. It failed to mention they are a normal physical attribute for women—and men—to carry, even the super in-shape women and men.

I got home late in the evening and laid the cream and some plastic wrap out on the bed.

"What are you doing?" Rosie asked.

Less than ten minutes later, I had cellulite cream massaged into my skin, tightly compressed by layers of plastic wrap on my thighs and stomach. It was supposed to take away the appearance of cellulite and make you look slimmer, I told her.

Soon, Janie was in the room too and we were all laughing at how ridiculous I looked and how silly of a method it was.

They may not have thought it would make a difference, yet deep down I truly believed it would.

When I took the plastic wrap off and looked in the mirror, I swore I saw less cellulite and a thinner stomach. After this night, I continued to lather on the cream and wrap my body with plastic.

Looking back at pictures now, I had little to no cellulite and my stomach was not fat, yet body dysmorphia invaded my life. Staring in the mirror for hours at a time and seeing everything except for reality.

Body dysmorphia is more commonly known as body dysmorphic disorder, or BDD, and is a mental health disorder that causes an individual to obsess over their appearance. They cannot escape the perceived flaws they notice in themselves and will sometimes spend hours body checking in front of the mirror, trying to "fix" what they see as broken. Some will go as far as avoiding social situations or having cosmetic procedures done. BDD is not a normal recognition of flaws; it is an intense focus on something that is not there or is not nearly as noticeable as the individual sees it.[36]

I was never diagnosed with BDD but won't ever forget writing a letter to my mom when I was younger asking her to *please* help me get plastic surgery done on my lady parts I thought were disfigured. I expressed how I couldn't go on living my life with the belief I was damaged. Only, I never gave her the letter because I was afraid she'd start to believe I was damaged, too.

It is this kind of distorted perception that continued to fuel my efforts during my eating disorder to lose weight. I didn't know how I was going to do it but kept Googling ideas and running after practice in the meantime.

Then, the spring of freshman year, I got talked into trying out long-distance running during track season. I originally started out as a thrower, and after just one practice running, I decided to sign up for the 1500-meter event. If you don't know how far 1500 meters is, it's about 3.75 laps around a normal 400-meter track, as fast as you can.

The 1500-meter run was and is hard, but I *loved* it. I still remember the feeling I had when turning one of the corners of the track and thinking, *Holy crap, I'm going to puke.*

Seeing that I didn't throw up and ended up doing quite well, I found myself signing up for the 1500-meter race again, and again, and again.

---

36 "Body Dysmorphic Disorder," Accessed October 6, 2020.

I fell in love with distance running so much I quit volleyball and started running with the cross country team the summer I moved in with Rosie. I was turning my one-mile run into seven, ten, sometimes thirteen-mile runs.

I found out quickly running was one of the gifts I never knew I had. I loved how friendly fellow runners were, the mental shift I got from the "runner's high," and the fact I was good at it.

However, in time, it became clear my love for cross country was less about the sport and more about the idea that with so much running, I might be able to shrink myself and stop obsessing so much over my body image—what I thought was the root of so many of my problems.

I look back now and realize deep down my love for running was intertwined with the belief who I was—just as I was— was not worthy.

The way I felt and sometimes still feel about my exterior is only a symptom of something deeper, a symptom of being wounded more than once, and a symptom of believing lies about my identity.

A big part of my disordered eating sprouted from a false interpretation of what beauty and success look like, and even more so it sprouted from lies about who I was and who I'd be if I wasn't able to maintain the ideal beauty image. It's deeper. It's a narrative twisted around so many of our culture's ideas that to untwist it takes a very long time.

To deal with the interior often meant turning to the exterior because, amid excess circumstances that felt miles away from my grip, changing my body image felt within my control, if only slightly.

I wanted to change what I saw on the outside because I hated what I felt on the inside and clung to the false idea if I could just be skinny, all my problems would disappear. I now know it's acknowledging and sharing our inwardness that keeps us safe.

Take this quote from Mark Nepo for example:

> You must meet the outer world with your inner world or existence will crush you. If inner does not meet outer, our lives will collapse and vanish. Though we often think that hiding our inwardness will somehow protect or save us, it is quite the opposite. The heart is very much like a miraculous balloon. Its lightness comes from staying full. Meeting the day with our heart prevents collapse.[37]

Believing a perfect body is enough to sustain life's challenges is a lie many of the men and women in our world still believe. As I continue sharing my eating disorder story, I hope you find yourself a little less susceptible to normalized thoughts and behaviors surrounding beauty.

---

37   Nepo, *The Book of Awakening*, 32-33.

Instead, ask the questions:

How do I define beauty and has my definition been influenced by the world?

How does God define beauty and how can I better align my thoughts with His?

If I or someone around me is struggling with eating disorder thoughts or behaviors, what is one thing I want myself or them to know?

CHAPTER 11

LOVABLE

"The more we depress, the more we push down and keep in, the smaller we become. The more we stuff between our heart and our daily experience, the more we have to work through to feel life directly. Our unexpressed life can become a callus we carry around and manicure, but never remove."

—MARK NEPO[38]

After moving in with my grandparents, I had a choice over the food I ate for the first time. My grandma asked me what I usually had for breakfast, what I wanted to pack in my lunches for school, and what kind of meals I preferred for dinner.

Since running cross country, I'd been given access to other runner's lives, what they were eating, and how much they were eating. I started taking mental notes and told Grandma I'd tag along with her to the store.

---

38 Nepo, *The Book of Awakening*, 52.

Some of the items I picked out included rice cakes, trail mix, granola bars, fruit, yogurt, carrots, whole grain bread, turkey, and apples. All items I associated with being "healthy."

I couldn't wait to pack my lunch and have more control over what I ate each day, so I started planning. I would have an apple and peanut butter for breakfast, a turkey sandwich with carrots for lunch, some trail mix or yogurt for a snack, and a granola bar before practice. Everything was neatly spaced out in my head, as I liked it.

Dinner was never later than six and would be ready when I got home from cross country. Knowing Grandma, there would be a veggie, potatoes or rice, some sort of meat, bread, and *always* dessert.

I dreamt about dinner with my grandparents all day. So much so that when I first began eating with them, one of the comments made by my grandma was, "The food isn't going anywhere, Carly. You can slow down."

But I couldn't help it. During a long ten-mile run, my motivation to run faster was the thought of piping hot food set out on the table to enjoy and feast on in my new home.

Grandma was constantly introducing new vegetables I hadn't ever tried like beets and Brussel sprouts, and she always made them taste *so good*. She would laugh whenever I asked her what something was, like sweet potatoes. My gosh, did sweet potatoes change my life!

The bottom line: dinner with Grandma and Grandpa was my favorite time of the day. Sharing a meal with them felt like home, and although I did get to experience dinners around the table when I lived with Rosie, there was something unique about my grandparents' house that made me feel more like a resident than a visitor.

At Rosie's, I knew my time there was only temporary. I wasn't living with my dad, yet I was still dealing with court hearings, lawyers, and countless phone calls.

When I moved in with my grandparents, there was a sense of permanency. The battle was won. I had been given my own room to put my belongings in, the consistency of knowing what to expect each day, and family who I was deeply loved by.

Grandpa was retired and Grandma still worked, and going from being empty nesters for years to adding another child into the mix was exciting for them, too, I'm sure. They had walked by my side through the pain I encountered living with my dad, and to see me set free from his care and in their hands was a blessing to all of us.

The memory I have of my grandma in the journal entry below is my absolute favorite:

October 1st, 2013
Living with grandma and grandpa couldn't be better. I love it and I look forward to coming home every day. It's so relaxing, and I love having my own space. Grandma came into my room today, climbed up on my bed, kissed me, and told me how happy she was about me living here. She does so much.

Determined to Keep Running

Although things were going amazing with my grandparents after moving in, I was still receiving random calls from my dad, which all ended in disappointment, tears, guilt, and anger.

I knew leaving my dad's home would cause him pain at first, but I still believed a day would come where he'd be able to look at the situation from afar and understand why I did what I did.

He will understand I was only trying to protect myself.
He will see I was after safety and a home where I felt cared for and heard.
He will take ownership over the places he's fallen short as a parent.
He will come to accept and acknowledge his drinking problem and the scars it has caused those around him.
We can and one day will restore our relationship.

With each conversation, however, my hope for these things diminished.

I'd come in from talking on the phone outside, and my grandma would follow me into my room. I didn't have to say anything.

She knew between every spiteful comment and dig he made, I tried to get in everything I wanted to say to clean up the mess. She knew by my tears and the look in my eyes, I believed I caused the mess. Leaving was supposed to fix things, yet all it seemed to do was ruin them even more.

He said he couldn't ever forgive me.
He said I only had two more years. I could have toughed it out and then done whatever I wanted.
Why am I so weak?
Look at all the trouble I've caused.
All those things he did for me... he made sacrifices for me.
He's right. I was just sensitive and overreacted.
I thought this was the right thing to do, but now my own dad wants nothing to do with me.
Is this all my fault?

"Carly, I don't think these phone calls are healthy for you to keep having. You didn't do anything wrong," Grandma would say.

I soon stopped answering the phone when my dad called. I had to quit hoping the next time would be better, and I needed to set boundaries to protect myself. Still, accepting my dad and I might not ever have a relationship again was a hard concept to swallow.

It wasn't just my dad who didn't want a relationship with me. His parents weren't talking to me, either. As I said earlier, none of them came to my high school graduation the year after this.

What made it even harder is my grandparents on my dad's side were not the type of grandparents you only see on holidays or at funerals. They were a big part of my life growing up.

Without my mom there, my grandma was a maternal figure who understood a lot of what my dad didn't. I'd call my grandma when I felt sick at school, and she'd come to pick me up, take me to her house, and get a comfy spot ready for me to settle into on the couch.

My grandpa and I were also very close in my younger years. He'd sit me on his lap and let me drive through the country roads (as long as I didn't tell Grandma).

I'd make him sit at the dinner table the whole time Grandma cooked just so I could take his order and play waitress, bringing him more beverages than he asked for and delivering the check afterward. He always played along and made sure to leave a tip.

I loved spending time with the two of them, like getting up early to go on walks and collect seashells whenever we'd have family trips to the beach. Staying up late, eating M&M's, and playing Skip-Bo. I loved Grandma's waffles, the smell of the hand soap in the bathroom, and how the beds there always felt like soft clouds.

However, I had to erase memories like this from my mind when both my dad and my grandparents could not forgive me for moving out.

The whole situation left me feeling an assortment of emotions I never slowed down to process. Instead, I sped up to forget.

Running was the place I did this the most. All it took after an emotional phone call with my dad was running down the country roads outlining fields and houses for miles and miles to forget the pain I was feeling. Music blaring. Rain or shine.

It wasn't so much the coping strategy writing is for me. Writing forces me to name and process my feelings. To write them out on paper and close the journal afterward is cathartic. Running, on the other hand, is what I did to feel in control when I had so many emotions rushing through me I felt paralyzed. I couldn't write them down and didn't want to because they scared me. The feelings were too heavy, and I needed to do something to get outside of myself.

I hated who I was because who I was didn't seem to be enough. Cross country—what started as a hobby and something I enjoyed—soon became a discipline. The chaos and monsters in my head wouldn't leave, so I tried to leave them.

If I could just turn the music up loud enough.

If I could just wake up to run before they woke, I could have some peace.

If I could just perfect my run, completing the number of miles I said I was going to complete while not cutting any corners.

Maybe then my monsters wouldn't say anything. If I could just shrink myself, I wouldn't feel so out of place.

Maybe then someone would love me. Maybe then I would love me.

For a while, there was an image God kept bringing to mind. An image of me running on a country road, one that is familiar and used to be incorporated into many of my routes.

While I was running on the country road aiming to hit a certain destination, I was simultaneously running away from many things that scared and pained me terribly.

Each time God brings this image to mind, it's when I feel distant from Him. My sense is He's trying to tell me I'm running the wrong way from feelings and events I find too heavy to carry, or from anger and hurt I think don't have the energy to process.

Running away from feelings is not a new tactic of mine, however, it's one I'm far more aware of now than when I was in high school.

I know now God is only a breath away. I always have access to His peace and know whenever I do feel distant or He feels quiet, it's more a loose wire on my end than on His.

Knowing this, I still need simple reminders and images to pull me away from the noise of my mind and this world, and to show me a much better route.

My first season of cross country eventually came to an end, and although many of my friends on the team couldn't wait to have a break from practice and races, I already had an entire running schedule put together.

'm not stopping now! Basketball is just around the corner, and I'm taking full advantage of my time off!

So many people had positively affirmed my running abilities and the weight loss that had come with it up to that point. They were telling me I had slimmed up and looked great, asking, *How did you do it? It can't just be the running!*

Soon, my love for running escalated into unhealthy patterns of excessive weight loss, obsession with food, and exercise addiction.

A Life of Rules

In the beginning days of my eating disorder, the weight loss I experienced wasn't extremely unhealthy. I had only lost around ten pounds, and although I was slimmer and people did notice, most of the things I was doing were deemed normal: drinking large amounts of water, not eating two hours before bed, avoiding sugar, eating smaller portions with lots of fruits and vegetables.

At most, I got called a "health nut." Once basketball began, my team would laugh at how frequently I had to go to the bathroom. They'd make jokes when I decided to get the salad instead of a burger after a game, and occasionally said something to the extent of how I needed to, "Put meat on my bones."

Their laughs and comments didn't bother me and, if anything, only validated my actions and made me want to continue following my rules. Of course, I made it seem my actions were nothing more than instincts. What those around me didn't know, however, is almost all my actions were based on numbers.

Most days, I aimed to drink seven twenty-four-ounce water bottles before the evening. The number I read on the scale determined what foods ranked as acceptable and non-acceptable. Serving sizes were never ignored. I'd count the crunchy chips in my mouth one by one, wondering how the other girls on my team could eat whatever they wanted and not gain weight.

The items I selected at the grocery store with Grandma started to fall under an even more precise list. If someone offered me food, I'd still grab at it, but as I ate, I'd be calculating calories, sugar, and what I'd need to do later to feel okay about eating the food.

This behavior carried into my dinners with Grandma and Grandpa, too. I could still enjoy our time around the table, but I'd need to keep following my rules.

As long you make sure veggies are the most present thing on your plate, you can have potato. But watch out for the starch!

One small piece of bread is okay but only a thumbnail of butter. Too much and you might have a heart attack.

If the meat is lighter, it is better for you. Dark meat is full of fat. Don't eat a lot of it.

Only water with dinner. Good job, never drink your calories.

Try to avoid dessert, and if you feel tempted, eat a piece of fruit or chew gum.

I didn't want other people to notice how much I planned, analyzed, and calculated the food I ate and became very good at playing things cool.

Making it seem like eating ice cream or French fries was no big deal, then tacking on three miles to my weekend run to pay for it, or taking laxatives when I got home to get rid of the food.

Lying to say I was full anytime I did turn down food offered to me, because I knew accepting it came with an expensive price tag.

Saying I loved food too much to ever go on a diet, while hiding the fact I'd had nothing but two rice cakes and a banana just so I could enjoy some pizza with my friends on the weekend.

I'd laugh when others told me I was so skinny and could eat whatever I wanted, all while in my head thinking, *If only they knew what I had to do to be okay with eating this pizza.*

I kept my disordered behaviors quiet the rest of my junior year of high school, mainly my intake of laxatives. The other things I was doing to lose weight may have been excessive, though I never would have admitted to having an eating disorder.

No, what I'm doing is healthy.
The weight loss magazines say so.
The internet says so.

The shows I watched on Netflix say so.
Even my friends and my family have said so.

Rules kept me safe.

If I had carrots earlier in the day, I'd better not have them later in the day. If the protein bar I grabbed in the morning to eat before practice was peanut butter flavor, I wouldn't eat it because, *duh, stupid. You had peanut butter with an apple for breakfast.*

If I broke my rules, I was bad. It was as simple as that.

Soon summer arrived, and I had coffee with my grandparents before going running. We'd talk about the day ahead and wake up slowly together before each doing our own thing.

My mom's dad is sadly no longer with us yet managed to fill his day with a project until the day of his passing. He made just about every piece of furniture in my grandparents' home and still is an inspiration to many, including me. Whenever you had a question on how to do something, all you had to do was ask Papa. He always had an answer. If he didn't, he wouldn't stop thinking about it until he did.

Years ago, he found a niche turning scrap pieces of metal into breathtaking trees, and his last project involved putting together his second model ship with thousands of pieces. We framed the unfinished product, and seeing it always reminds me to never give up.

On a typical day, Grandma would follow Grandpa down to the shop after getting ready. Rather than building, she would instead be quilting with some country music on low and hard candy nearby.

Disordered Relationships

The summer after my junior year, I had finally stopped receiving calls from my dad and tried my hardest to put him in the back of my mind. It hurt too much to think about, and most days I just wouldn't let myself go there. Other days, the thought of him would eat me alive.

That was the same summer I met Kasey. My relationship with Kasey is a story worth telling because he is one of the main people who helped me forget about the brokenness in my family.

We still stay in touch and think back to that summer as one we won't ever forget.

Nearly every day was spent together swimming, kissing, stargazing, and laughing. We laughed so much it would take us an hour to say goodbye some nights because of how silly we were being.

As summer came to an end, we continued dating, and I started my second year of cross country, which called for two weeks of daily doubles. That's one practice in the morning and one in the evening, and it's exhausting. Still, some days I'd get in my car right after our morning practice ended to drive over to his house forty minutes away.

My relationship with Kasey was the first real relationship I had been in that was easy. We never fought. We never faced drama. I got along with his friends, and he got along with mine. What we had was beautiful, yet my preoccupation with food and exercise lingered.

You see, he wasn't just in shape, he had a full-on six-pack, which remained chiseled without flexing. He had a gym at his house, worked out regularly, and was an amazing pole vaulter.

I'd be lying if I said I didn't face insecurity when around him. Sure, I ran more miles than he'd ever be willing to run—I know this because he called me crazy every time I showed up after practice and told him how far I ran—yet I still made up stories in my head about what kind of girl he liked.

Surely, he wanted someone with more muscle definition. Surely, he wanted a girl who didn't eat as much food as I did—a girl who didn't get so excited about pizza and cereal. I worried about what he thought when I was eating.

One night I boxed up my food at the restaurant we were at so he wouldn't see me eating more than I already had. Then, later that night, I finished it in the car on my way home. I didn't have utensils, so I used my fingers. *I couldn't wait.*

I don't remember if I was actually hungry or if I was doing nothing more than searching to satisfy a deeper craving of my soul. All I know is my monsters consistently told me I had to be someone else to be loved. Never mind what I was craving. Never mind my hunger. There were people to impress and I better not disappoint.

It seemed my food rules and runs just weren't getting the job done quick enough. I needed to go to more extremes, my monsters told me.

Cross country was sucking up all of my time, and it wasn't enjoyable anymore. Coach was sending me out to run with the varsity guys during practice because I was improving quickly, but by the end of each run, I'd end up alone because I was faster than most of the girls and slower than most of the guys.

On top of that, my body was exhausted, and I was dealing with minor knee and Achilles tendon pain. Coach said to make sure I stretched and told me the only race he cared about me doing well in was districts.

I think he was more determined than we were to get to state, and it showed when a majority of the team was lying on the turf complaining of feeling sick and said they were about to pass out. I was too competitive to ever slow down or stop running when I was in pain, however, I remember one race in particular where I had to stop and walk.

The week before, we had put in nearly sixty miles with not one day off before our race on Saturday, and then on Saturday, we were expected to run a trail with all sorts of hills in upper seventy-degree weather. I felt I was carrying a trailer of bricks behind me.

I didn't agree with my coach's rationale: beat us down to build us up.

What is the point of this? I don't want to hate every race of the season and feel like crap just so I can maybe run well for one race. This isn't why I signed up for cross country.

There was so much pressure, and I felt obligated to live up to an expectation I didn't believe I could meet. Looking back, this could have been due to my need for perfection combined with the harsh coaching style. In *The Road Back to You*, Ian Morgan Cron and Suzanne Stabile discuss what it's like to be a One on the Enneagram under stress. For me, this explains much of what I was feeling at the time.

> In stress, Ones instinctively take on the not-so-great qualities we'd expect to see in unhealthy Fours (the Individualists). Their inner critic begins working overtime, and their need to perfect the world goes into overdrive. They become more resentful of others having fun, more sensitive to criticism, and depressed. In this space, they long to be free of obligations and responsibilities, lose confidence, and feel unlovable.[39]

The next week, I wrote a letter and met with my coach to tell him I was quitting.

My monsters told me I didn't need to be on a team to reach my goals. Now I could run when I wanted to. They said I'd have more freedom and choice.

---

39 Ian Morgan Cron and Suzanne Stabile, *The Road Back to You: An Ennea-gram Journey to Self-Discovery* (Westmont: InterVarsity Press, 2016), 107.

Except when I quit running cross country, I faced even more depletion because they *never* let me rest.

I started monitoring my food even closer and experienced a heavy sense of shame any time I ate, and I didn't run because, up until that point, running was one of the major ways I got rid of food.

Another thing to add to my stress was more time and less obligations. I've learned a blank schedule and I don't get along because I get overwhelmed with choice, try to fit too much into one day, and freeze up when anxiety strikes. This phenomenon is great for my monsters because it allows them even more control in making me do things I don't actually feel like doing. They deprive me of intuition and before I know it, I have a full schedule again.

Your Vice Becomes Your Friend

What I came to believe about running is without it I wouldn't be myself. I'd be irritable and hard to be around. The reason why is because food and exercise were my coping strategies to deal with many of the underlying emotions I found horrifying. Unlike drinking or smoking, I just so happened to be addicted to two things often seen as positive additions to one's life, and it was hard to draw the line between what was acceptable and what wasn't.

We all have ways of coping, some healthy, some unhealthy, and some that start healthy but eventually become unhealthy. And to let go of our coping mechanisms is troublesome when they have, time and time again, helped us overcome adversity.

Even when, to an outsider, the addiction is doing nothing more than ruining a person's life, it has very well become that person's friend.

You will see later, after discovering I was indeed suffering a mental illness, it took over a year to commit to recovery because my eating disorder made me feel safe and I couldn't imagine a life without it.

I want to continue with my story but first want to say that if you're struggling with an addiction to food and exercise, you are accepted. I accept you, God accepts you, and I hope you learn to accept yourself because you, dear friend, are lovable.

CHAPTER 12

NOT SKINNY ENOUGH

I feel so caught up. My head is pounding. I want to curl up in a ball and do nothing. I wish that in real life there were timeouts so that when things got tough you could say, "Hey, you know... I don't really like this feeling—timeout!" And then when you felt calm and ready, you could say, "Okay, Coach, put me back in." But life doesn't work that way, and I'm tired.

At first, things were great after quitting cross country. Then, in the blink of an eye, I spiraled even further into disordered eating.

I thought because I wasn't running, I didn't need as many carbohydrates as before. I believed I *should* be more restrictive because I wasn't performing for anyone. If I chose not to run, it was okay, but only if I also chose not to eat.

I'm running as many miles as before, so I can get by on less food.

To replace the time I spent at practices and races, I started working and hanging out with Kasey more. At one point, I was working three jobs. On top of that, I was involved in nearly eight clubs and extracurriculars at school to try and "make the most of my time." I still hadn't learned it was okay to say no and committed my attention to so many different things because they all—to some extent—mattered to me.

Kasey mattered; he reminded me to laugh. My jobs mattered because I was determined to pay for college. Every club and volunteer experience mattered; they allowed me to lead and give back to those around me. I was fixated on "making a difference" and wanted to do something meaningful with my time in high school, only I got lost along the way.

Soon after my senior year of high school started, I dealt with horrible migraines almost every day. Kasey and I would meet up after I'd gone hours without eating and all I'd do is complain. I didn't feel good. I had no appetite, and I was always tired.

The night of homecoming, we went to the football game and dance, and after being inside for only five minutes, I insisted on going out to the truck. My head hurt too bad, I told him. I needed to close my eyes.

So, he went back inside and danced while I slept outside in the truck. I stayed over once the dance had reached its end. Not for any funny business, but because I felt too sick to drive home.

That wasn't the only night my migraines interfered with time spent with Kasey. I felt bad, mostly for him, yet wouldn't admit it until after breaking up.

We had gone from a summer filled with highs and being super connected to drifting apart. We had a summer full of adventure and fun. Now, I wasn't any fun at all. I started to notice our distance, and instead of talking to him about it, I mistakenly interpreted the distance as his disinterest. I started to self-sabotage.

If he can't like me now—while I don't feel well and am not constantly upbeat—how will our relationship ever last?

Instead of putting myself in his shoes, I stood strong in mine. *Poor me. This always happens. I should have known this was too good to be true.*

Kasey and I came to a mutual agreement that things between us were different than at the start of our relationship. When he suggested talking about it, I told him there was nothing to talk about. It was over. The truth is, I feared he only wanted to explain in person why he was breaking up with me, and I couldn't handle that.

All of my friends were surprised we had broken up, and when they asked why, I kept my responses vague because I couldn't bear the shame of admitting it was mostly due to my health complications and lack of enthusiasm. I was a drag to be around.

My monsters clapped their hands knowing I was no longer a part of a team and I no longer had a boyfriend, two major support systems in my life at that time. All that was left to destroy was my relationships with my three best friends, which were already dwindling and had been since July before I met Kasey.

July 5, 2014
Last night I got in a fight with the girls. I yelled at them and they yelled at me. Is it wrong that I'm not okay with all of my friends attacking me at once? I'm sure I'm not the only person who doesn't enjoy getting told everything that they're failing at. My issue is that I know I'm doing things wrong, and I know I need help. I guess it just hurts knowing that I'm not the only one aware of my many issues.

Knowing others could see my "flaws" caused me to shut down. I hated hearing what I was doing wrong because I already faced such a harsh inner critic. I'd get lost thinking what I might do to prove myself worthy.

Do I find myself in these episodes of silence because I'm angry with my many problems and don't want to share that ugliness with others? Or is it because I realize my problems, yet ignore them by putting on a pretty face and acting like everything's okay because I'm afraid others just won't get it? I don't want those around me to suffer from the emotions that are already drowning me.

It seemed I was in the middle of nowhere without a map. I wanted to change and not be so unsettled by my emotions and struggled to express to my friends how I was feeling whenever they asked. It was like I was losing my mind.

I'm scatterbrained and tired—tired of never knowing. Maybe I'm upset because my dad doesn't want anything to do with me.

Maybe I'm sad because I just found out that my grandpa, who I haven't spoken to in months, now has cancer. I might even be mad that my face is breaking out. I wouldn't know. But I've been told to never stop writing... even when writing becomes hard and you feel stuck. So, here's my attempt to write through the toughness—something I'd say I'm pretty experienced at.

Making friends wasn't hard for me and still isn't. It's keeping them that is hard. Having friends is not easy. Toward the end of summer when I could sense my relationship coming to an end with Rosie and my other two best friends, I decided I would leave them before they left me. It was like breaking up with Kasey all over again.

I don't need friends who judge and yell at me every time I'm not 100 percent present. Don't they know what I'm going through?

The answer was no, they didn't, because I never told them.

The night we got into a fight, I expected them to have compassion for me while catering to everything I was going through. I was hoping the night would be more about me and my problems.

When they didn't respond the way I hoped, I shut down. I gave them the silent treatment and would blame my numbness on something they did because I couldn't accept the fact I was depressed and deeply affected by my depression. Every time I did, I had the voice of my dad in my head telling me I was overreacting and being a drama queen.

On the other hand, they had expectations for me to show up and join in on the Fourth of July celebration. We were at a firework show on a warm sunny night. *Why would we talk about Carly's problems? Why would we turn this fun night into a sad one?* When I became a stick in the mud and they noticed my mood, they became combative.

The rest of the summer and heading into my senior year, I rarely spoke to the three of them. I knew we'd eventually need to get over the tiff we had that night but I wasn't about to turn the other cheek and neither were they. Instead, we continued having awkward exchanges.

When Kasey and I were still dating, I convinced myself I didn't mind not having my three best friends because I had him. Plus, I made new friends. *I'm good,* I told myself. Only I wasn't because when we broke up, I was dealing with the loss of him, my friends, the entire cross country team, and a major father wound.

Who am I and why am I all of a sudden alone?
It's better that way, my monsters would say.

I soon convinced myself it was better. I had so much more time to focus on getting in even *better* shape, improving my diet, and excelling in school.

Soon enough, I'd be going off to college anyway. Nothing was holding me back, and I was willing to do everything I could to leave the dingy town I grew up in.

Rejecting All Concern and Care

It was Saturday and I woke up first thing to run. After putting in five miles on the treadmill, I showered and made a list of all I planned to accomplish that weekend.

I drank some coffee and headed out the door for work when my grandma caught me and reached out with an egg sandwich, one of my favorites. I turned down her offer because part of my plan that day included not eating bread. Plus, I told her I had already eaten a fruit and nut bar. I wasn't hungry.

She set down the napkin holding the sandwich and looked at me with concern. "Carly, I'm worried about you. You're doing too much, and I don't think you're eating enough."

Another afternoon, I rushed home from school to get a run in before my evening shift at one of my jobs. I ran as far as I could in the time I had between school and work, which ended up being about three miles, what I considered a short run at the time.

Afterward, I showered, and when I headed out to my car, I ran into both my mom and grandma. I didn't realize anyone else was home and learned they had been down in the shop chatting in my grandma's quilting studio.

"Where are you off to?" my mom asked.

Grandma shook her head with disappointment and walked into the house.

"I have work," I said.

My mom proceeded to tell me she wished she could have spent time with me. When she came up to the house, I was busy running. I told her I was sorry, life was just busy. She then asked what I ate that day.

"Can I send you with something for dinner?"

I told her I wasn't hungry and had to leave or else I would be late.

As I pulled out of the driveway, I was afraid to look up because I knew if I did, her eyes would be there to meet mine with nothing more than concern and confusion.

I used to feel physically sick after I ran because I would push myself too hard. I'd lose any appetite I had before running and sometimes just wouldn't eat the rest of the day because I felt no sign of hunger. My stomach had a tightness to it, a constant burning sensation I grew to rely on. If I didn't feel it, I was under the belief I didn't work hard enough.

I'd get home after chewing gum and drinking water my whole shift to find a plate of dinner left for me by the stove. Grandma would already be in bed, and Grandpa was usually out on the living room floor playing solitaire or dozing off between episodes of *I Love Lucy*.

Some nights I'd eat the veggies and throw the rest of the food away underneath the other garbage to avoid hurting Grandma's feelings. Other times, I'd get upset if she left me a plate of food because of the obligation I felt to eat past my set eating hours. I'd leave it in the fridge untouched.

Didn't she know it would be too late for me to eat when I got home?
Why is she so obsessed with making me fat?
Could she stop leaving food out for me? Damnit, it stresses me out!
I don't want to eat, but I don't want to hurt her.

Except I did her hurt her. I hurt so many of the people around me by trying to achieve and do more in an attempt to be perfect. It seemed my world was made of glass and if I just kept the outside clean, I could trick people into thinking the inside was too.

The Best and Most Challenging Year

After I turned eighteen, my grandparents sat me down and said they thought it would be a good idea for me to go and live with my mom for the last bit of time before I went off to college. At that moment, I was completely opposed.

No way.
This is my home.
That would be my third move in less than two years.
I don't want to leave.
What about our dinners?
I love it here.
I'm used to it here.

It took some prompting. However, my grandparents were right when they said it would mean everything to my mom and me.

She and I had waited ten years for the moment no one told us we couldn't be together, and my dad and the courts had no authority.

Still, I was hesitant to move because of how perfect my grandparents' home ended up being. It was noisy at my mom's with both my siblings there. Her boyfriend was kind of messy and acted like a child at times. I had a room there, yet it wasn't technically my room. It was more like a guest room I got to sleep in when I was there.

I shouldn't have doubted my mom's abilities to ease the concerns I had because, within two weeks, she had built me a walk-in closet, turned my little sister's room into my room (much bigger than the guest room), and made it homier than I had ever imagined. There was so much detail, so much love.

Living with my mom was positive in its own way until the past resentment I mentioned earlier arose.

I look back and I am ashamed at how I treated my mother, the person who gave me life and helped me walk on my own two feet. My eating disorder behaviors worsened when I was living with her because of how much stress I was under, and because of how much I relied on things like food to make it all better.

I'd stand over her as she made dinner, asking about every ingredient that went into the food. I'd get furious when she put unnecessary amounts of oil or butter into things. I hated when my foods repeated, and my mom never seemed to understand.

"Why are you putting cheese in there? Can't we have it on the side?" I'd ask her.
"What's the big deal?" she'd respond.
"I already had cheese today!"
"You had cream cheese..."
"It's still cheese, and you know I only like to have one serving of cheese a day!"
"I barely put any in, Carly."
"You don't need that much oil for the vegetables!"
"Carly, knock it off. A little cheese and oil aren't going to hurt you."
"You don't get it. Whatever, I just won't eat."

Only, I would eat, and there would be consequences afterward. One of my favorite meals my mom used to make was grilled burritos with rice, beans, chicken, tomato, cheese, and avocado. She'd crisp them to perfection, and when you bit into one, there'd be a string of cheese hanging down your lip.

The day I found out she was making burritos for dinner, I barely ate anything. I couldn't wait. Then, when dinner came, I ate eight of them within minutes. I couldn't stop. I wanted to be done after three yet didn't feel I had a choice.

It was like I was possessed by an uncontrollable hunger that couldn't be satisfied through food. Johnston says, "Many women do not recognize the addictive nature of disordered eating until they find themselves in the throes of it, mercilessly driven by a compulsion for thinness and hounded by an appetite for food that seems insatiable."[40]

I kept eating and eating, to the point where the food didn't even taste good anymore. Afterward, I went and put my running clothes on and ran eight miles, a mile for every burrito.

In his book *Personality Types*, Don Richard Riso explains this behavior well. He says:

Unhealthy Ones now become obsessed (neurotically preoccupied) with whatever has become their focus of fury, but which, because of their need to control themselves, they cannot act upon directly. As a result, they act compulsively, controlled more than ever by their irrational impulses... Obsessive thoughts go repeatedly through their minds... The intensity of their obsessions may be so troubling to neurotic Ones that they may feel possessed by demons. In a certain sense, neurotic Ones are "possessed," although their demons are the repressed feelings and impulses they have not allowed themselves to deal with.[41]

He goes on to say that for unhealthy Ones, food can be a way to cope with obsessions about the body, which could result in anorexia or bulimia.[42]

---

40   Johnston, *Eating in the Light of the Moon*, 34.
41   Riso, *Personality Types*, 293-294.
42   Riso, *Personality Types*, 294.

Hiding From a Truth I Couldn't See

I was standing in my room trying on dresses for a formal one day, and my friend Hannah was over. As I changed into dress after dress, she asked me how I'd lost so much weight.

She was asking for her own benefit, and I did the thing I always did and played it cool as I listed off a few of the "natural" ways I had lost weight.

"I just run a lot, eat super healthy, and don't eat two hours before bed," I'd say.

My mom came in the room shortly after to see what we were up to and to hand over a couple more dresses I might consider wearing.

It was the first time my mom had seen me undressed for a while, and I remember her eyes being planted on my body as she voiced out loud I was "too skinny."

As I pulled up one of the dresses, she told me she could see my ribs and collarbone coming through my skin. Hannah added how she never thought I needed to lose weight in the first place.

I stood in front of my full-length mirror in a small pink dress, my mom behind me and Hannah to my side. I looked in the mirror, and for a second, it was just me and my body. And I wanted to feel sorry for it. I wanted to see what both of them saw, but I couldn't. The more I stared, the more flaws I found.

Too skinny? What is she talking about?

All I saw in that mirror was a fat, useless body that did nothing more than bring me trouble. My monsters encouraged and validated these thoughts.

There's still weight to lose.
You aren't done yet.
You can't trust people, not even the ones who claim to love you.

I got dressed, ashamed for even thinking I might be able to escape judgment by changing in front of two people closest to me.

Another night, I came home after one of my basketball games, crying uncontrollably. Coach had barely played me and each time he did, I got pulled out for the smallest mistake. I wasn't strong enough, he told me after the game.

It was a home game, and I was supposed to start and contribute. *So what if I made a mistake; doesn't everyone?* I was determined and willing to fix my mistakes, to try harder and do better, and it was obvious I was being given the smallest amount of grace on the court that night.

Later that evening, my mom came into my room to help me hang up the clothes I left out that morning on my bed. We sat in silence for a few minutes before she interrupted my sniffling nose to voice her concern for a second time.

"Carly, I sat behind you the other night at the team meeting, and it took everything in me to not cry at how visible your backbones were through your jersey. You don't look healthy. What are you doing with your food?"

I yelled back at her, "*Really, Mom?* Out of everyone to have accused me of having an eating disorder, I never thought you would be one of them. What do you mean, 'What am I doing with my food?' *I live with you.* You see me eat. You see me take lunch to school every day."

"I'm talking about after you eat. It just doesn't make sense, Carly. It wouldn't be right of me not to say something. As your mom, it is the hardest thing to watch your child harm themself."

"I can't believe this! I thought I could trust you! How many times have I come home and cried to you about how bullied I feel by those at school? Now you're turning your back on me, too?"

She walked over to my nightstand, opened the cabinet, and reached to the back. "Then what are these?" she asked, holding up a bottle of laxatives.

"They're laxatives, obviously. I barely use them. I forgot they were even there."

"The bottle was full less than a month ago, Carly."

"Oh, so now you're spying on me? That's just great, Mom. Get out of my room."

"Carly, you are beautiful. You have nothing to worry about."

She came over and placed her hands on my shoulders. "Shane, look at me."

Shane is my middle name and one only my mom gets away with using as my first name.

"What?"

"You are beautiful," she said again.

I didn't say anything.

"Please stop doing this to yourself," she went on. "You don't look healthy, and that's why people keep asking you what is going on. It's only because we care. I care. I'm not like everyone else. I'm your mom, and I want to see you gain a little weight back."

The room went from nothing but whispers to a raging yell.

"I am so done with all of this! Mom, you sat by my side as we waited for the results of the MRI. You backed me up when the neurologist said he couldn't find anything, and you insisted he run more tests. You know the migraines I've dealt with. You know how sick I get and how crappy I feel all the time. Stop accusing me! You're either on my side or you aren't!"

After that night, my mom rarely approached the topic again, and if she did, it was purely to let me know she was on my side. When she'd find out I got talked to by yet another teacher, staff member, or peer at school, she'd ask me if I wanted her to call and talk to them.

As I continued making doctors' appointments, she continued to either go with me or be in support of me going.

My mom chose to defend me because she was afraid of losing me again. To this day, she points to this as the reason why she never sent me to a recovery facility (something I wish she had done).

"I just couldn't. I thought you wouldn't ever forgive me."

Maybe it's true being sent to a recovery facility would have turned me away from my mom for a brief time, yet I don't think it would have lasted. Especially now, having understood the depth and cause of my eating disorder behaviors.

I think another reason my mom chose to defend me is that she truly believed me when I told her I didn't have a problem. I remember multiple instances when I lied to my dad or didn't tell him the entire story of a situation, but I can't think of one with my mom.

From the time I was a kid, I've always found her to be a safe place, and when I didn't tell her I had an eating disorder, it's because I didn't think I did. I didn't understand what an eating disorder was. This lack of knowledge and body dysmorphia caused me to think I wasn't skinny enough and, therefore, didn't have an eating disorder.

I wasn't throwing up; never once did I make myself throw up. I didn't starve myself for days. I ate—sometimes too much. Every image and idea I had of a woman with an eating disorder was so skewed I thought I surely wasn't one of those women. Little did I know there are various types of eating disorders.

A Lack of Education

I only remember learning about eating disorders once in the classroom before heading off to college. We were shown images of malnourished women who had anorexia, and within five minutes, we switched to a different topic.

The kids next to me were laughing about how stupid it was for someone to willfully not eat, and I sat there thinking how convenient it would be to have such strong willpower.

Nothing was said that day of the psychological effects an eating disorder can have on both the individual suffering and their family. Nothing was mentioned about the effects of media and how they influence the beauty ideal men and women hold.

Most people don't even know the sociocultural idealization of thinness is the number one environmental factor to contribute to the development of eating disorders.[43] Why? Because the toxic air it breeds has become normal.

Binge eating disorder, exercise addiction, avoidant/restrictive food intake disorder, orthorexia, bulimia, and the various

---

43   Kristen N. Culbert, Sarah E. Racine, and Kelly L. Klump, "Research Review: What We Have Learned about the Causes of Eating Disorders - a Synthesis of Sociocultural, Psychological, and Biological Research," *The Journal of Child Psychology and Psychiatry* 56, no. 11 (June 2015): 1141-1164.

other forms of eating disorders were not talked about, and even anorexia nervosa had missing gaps.

From my perspective, I found the brief (one slide only) presentation to make anorexia seem like a disorder from another planet only a slim number of people adopted. Maybe that's because I'm from a small town, or maybe it's because my teacher had limited knowledge of the topic.

Regardless, the scarce amount of information only led to misinformation, and I don't think I was the only student to walk away with an incomplete view of why and how someone develops an eating disorder.

Today, we are seeing more people open up about their disorders on social media, blogs, podcasts, and YouTube, especially during National Eating Disorder Awareness Week. Organizations like The Butterfly Foundation and National Eating Disorders Association offer resources to help inform and prevent the continuation of eating disorders.

Research has become more abundant over the years, and many brands are doing their part in exposing real people in their ads for clothing and beauty products. Examples of this are Third Love, American Eagle, Everlane, Dove, and more.

Still, we have a long way to go. Because up against the help, support, and stories from real people are *other* real people spreading diet culture like wildfire.

In the *Let's Thrive* podcast, my friend Emily Feikls interviewed Erin Christ on the "thin ideal" and diet culture.

During their conversation, Erin mentioned how today we live in a world fueled by the billion-dollar diet industry, which has caused obsession over both diets and changing our bodies to hopefully be "thin," and to avoid the fear of weight gain, being "fat," and failing to meet the beauty standard set before us.

> Diet culture has really done a really good job of worshiping this thinness and equating that to being healthy. It basically makes us believe that the only way for us to actually achieve good health and well-being and a high social status is by making our bodies smaller. It's so important to be able to challenge those messages and hopefully put an end to diet culture somewhat soon. It's essential to creating a world that's just and peaceful for people of all bodies.[44]

Looking back, I sometimes wonder if my story would have unfolded the way it did had I been better educated on the causes, symptoms, and treatment of eating disorders in a more welcoming and less shameful way.

Shame shuts people down. Even when I was in a place of not quite understanding the depth of eating disorders and my relationship to them, I was so embarrassed by how they were viewed and how I would be viewed that I couldn't allow myself any room to process or heal.

---

44 Erin Christ, "Weight Gain and the 'Thin' Ideal + Overcoming Diet Culture with Erin Christ," August 19, 2020, in *Let's Thrive,* produced by Emily Feikls, podcast, MP3 audio, 53:00.

I had all the signs and symptoms of an eating disorder, yet my mind couldn't get to that realization because of how big the ridicule and judgment blockade was.

I'd be in the shower and with only a light comb of my fingers, watch big masses of hair fall down the drain. I'd excuse the hair as "dead" because of how much I colored it.

My body would be covered in bruises, and I'd blame it on an intense basketball practice.

When my migraines started, I thought surely I had some sort of brain tumor or unknown health condition. I was always dizzy and tired.

I'd wear layers of sweaters to my summer job and say it was because of the air conditioning. Yet it didn't matter where I was. I was *always* cold.

People thought it was strange I had no menstrual cycle, but I assured them most lady runners don't.

The doctors would take my pulse three times because of how startling the low number was, and I assured them it was from running too.

I was so preoccupied with food, my body, and exercise because I thought they would provide me an escape from my monsters. My monsters even told me they would. They said all I needed to do was be in control, be better, be perfect, and then I would find peace. But I never found peace. Instead,

I found a lot of loneliness, insecurity, pain, and self-denial. There was *always* room for improvement.

The truth is, my eating disorder did serve me during difficult moments, but it wasn't meant to be a part of my life forever.

At some point, I needed to stop running away from my problems and instead run toward them. I know it sounds scary and, in the thick of our struggles, impossible. However, I've learned that until we confront our fears, we won't ever be satisfied.

What is it that *you* fear?
How are you coping with that fear?
If you could live life unafraid, what would you do?

Knowing what we fear is not enough; we have to go after that something. My first attempt at this was in my freshman year of college at Portland State University.

PART 3

REALIZATIONS AND TRANSFORMATIONS

CHAPTER 13

THE BEGINNING OF HEALING

___

"Having a mental illness doesn't mean you're weak. Just like someone with diabetes can choose to become physically strong, someone with depression can choose to become mentally strong."

—AMY MORIN[45]

I took a class during my freshman year of college called Family Communication. In it, I learned about eating disorders more in-depth and started to process my own. My professor, it turned out, understood just how much such illnesses affect not just the individual but the family.

I have never felt so revealed. As I sat in the front row of the lecture hall, I tried to keep my composure. All of a sudden, things started to click, like:

___

45 Morin, *13 Things Mentally Strong Women Don't Do*, 3.

The reason why I felt restricting my food or excessively exercising wasn't a choice.

The narratives I believed.

The pressure I felt to be better and to do better.

The anxiety.

The way I treated my mom.

All the times I canceled plans with friends.

All the times I felt buried in shame and unable to stop the cycle.

When I got back to my dorm room, I immediately called my mom to tell her I was sorry for the way I treated her in high school.

I told her I was coming to realize I did, in fact, have an eating disorder and didn't know it until then. I told her thank you for showing concern and loving me in the midst of it all, even though at times I treated her like my punching bag. She apologized for not doing more to help me and revealed her fear of losing or pushing me farther away if she did.

We had a beautiful conversation that ended with "I love you," and when I hung up the phone, I thought about all of the other people I should apologize to. The list was so long it overwhelmed me. And I wish I could say after our phone call I made amends with all of those people and recovered in full. Instead, I became obsessed with the different forms of eating disorders and felt I couldn't tell anyone else until I fully understood mine.

My family and friends thought I was doing much better because I had gained ten to fifteen pounds back from the thirty to forty I had lost in high school. Heck, *I thought I was doing better.*

It wasn't until further along in my journey I learned I still carried a lot of the same motives and behaviors.

Holding On When You're Afraid to Let Go

Through my recovery, I can confidently say it doesn't matter what you do to your physical appearance because until you've faced, dealt with, and handled your mental health, you will forever be held captive by something that deserves no authority in your life.

My disorder helped me cope, yes, but it also held me back from my true potential and passions.

It consumed so much of my time—planning when and what I would eat, stressing about when I would workout, analyzing and hating my body, completing calculation after calculation to try and figure out how much I needed to exercise to work off my food from the day before, spending hours in the kitchen preparing food I could bear less shame eating, having meal after meal alone just so I could avoid judgment from others.

These patterns became second nature, and because I gained weight and loosened up in a few areas, I rationalized them. But identifying my eating disorder was only one small step, and there were many leaps ahead I wasn't ready to take.

If you go online, you will find several pro-eating disorder websites telling people how to hide their disorder from their families and friends, how to better restrict, how to get rid of your food after mealtime, and more.

To many, this sounds insane, but as someone who has been in the dark depths of an eating disorder, I sort of get it. I never wanted to starve myself. I never wanted to binge. I never wanted to spend all day in the gym. Yet, at times, it seemed I didn't have a choice. The monsters in my head were so loud, so mean, and the only way to get rid of them was to obey their commands.

The temporary relief I felt when I did obey them fed my Type A, achieving mentality too much for me to let go. It made me feel like I was finally good at something, like I *was* good. Before I knew it, my eating disorder had become a part of me. It was mine! And who would I be if I were to let it go? I didn't know.

So, I gradually let recovery into some parts of my life but certainly not every part. This is another reason why I didn't want to tell anyone. I wasn't ready to be held accountable, and I wasn't ready to say goodbye.

I told myself the things I was doing weren't as intense as what I read online and learned in my class. They were things I did because I chose to.

You love running.
You eat healthy because it makes you feel good.
You're just a super independent person. Who cares if you cancel plans with friends?
You go to the gym to relieve stress.
You don't like sweet drinks; sugar-free tastes better to you.

These were *almost* true statements about me.

I loved running but not on injured knees or to the point of feeling sick.

I loved eating healthy 80 percent of the time, yet not when all of my friends were enjoying a piece of pie, and I had to lie and say I was too full to avoid the repercussions. I mostly liked to eat healthy because of the safe zone it kept me in.

I'm a super independent person, true, but I'm also a human who needs community and interaction with others just as much as everyone else.

I do go to the gym to relieve stress, yet I used to go for the primary reason of working off whatever food or drinks I had consumed. I went to the gym because I didn't believe I was worthy of love if I didn't.

I'm not the biggest fan of sweet beverages, but I used to be afraid of them because sugar was the first thing my eyes would look for on a food or drink label. To avoid being "bad," I would always choose the sugar-free option.

I remember one day my brother took a drink of the coffee I ordered and asked me, "Do you actually like that?" I lied and said I did, if only to convince myself I was happier with my decision than I was jealous of the whipped cream, chocolate-drizzled beverage he and my mom had chosen.

Naming Feelings

While learning more about my own eating disorder, and eating disorders as a whole, I started going to counseling because of the free services offered by my university. I didn't think I had a lot to work through. I'd just repeat my life story as I had so many times previously and probably be asked a few deep questions. It turned out I had a lot more brewing than I initially thought.

November 1, 2016
I need to be real about who I am. I need to be okay with who I am. That's something I'm struggling with right now, and my counselor is helping me work through it. I'm trying to become more vulnerable because I know that's a step toward achieving freedom, but it's so dang hard. I'm terrified to let people in… I wish I could just be happy with who I am. It feels like a constant battle trying to find myself. Maybe I'm looking in all the wrong places.

As my counselor Josh and I got away from the repetitive story of my past, we began crossing into new territory that required more openness from me.

One of the first things I learned about myself was I didn't know the difference between a feeling and thought. My counselor would always respond to things I spoke of by asking, "How does that make you feel?"

I would almost always respond with, "Well, I think..."

"Okay, but how does it make you feel?" he'd ask again.

"I think it makes me feel betrayed."

I'd label actions in my thoughts and call them "feelings." I was so out of touch with how I felt, I'd consistently let the rational part of my brain speak for me. I didn't want to deal with feelings because they were too messy.

But betrayal is not a feeling. It's an action that caused me to feel neglected, unwanted, used, trampled, and abused.

While writing this, I came across a homework assignment given to me by my counselor. The top of the sheet is titled *Emotion Words* and underneath the title are eleven categories of emotions.

My task was to take the sheet home and highlight all of the words I could begin to practice using in our sessions every time I was asked, "How does that make you feel?" It sounds easy, but it would take me five minutes to respond sometimes.

I was allowed my cheat sheet and would just sit there and stare at the words, so out of touch with how I felt that I could not respond. It was like there was a blockade keeping me from confronting my deeper emotions, a blockade that had been there for so long I thought it was keeping me safe, when really all it was doing was keeping me alone and fearful.

Working through the Ache

One day, Josh got me talking about my hometown, then high school, then about the eating disorder accusations thrown my way, and then about the friends I no longer spoke to. I could tell he wanted to dive deeper into the topic of eating disorders, but before he could, I told him the accusations were lies.

I told him the same story I had been telling myself about the migraines and the unknown health condition. I assured him I was feeling better and gained a lot of weight back.

"The doctor says I'm right where I'm supposed to be."

I was already sharing so much with him and wasn't ready to talk about something I had yet to understand myself.

Once he asked me, "Carly, do you ever cry?"
"Sometimes," I said. "Why?"
"Well, I've just noticed how you talk about some pretty intense events that have happened in your life, but you do so in such a calm way. I just want you to know you don't have to be strong here, and it is okay to cry."

I thanked him. I knew it was okay to cry, and I wished I could, yet so often I felt shut off from crying. No matter how much something hurt me, I couldn't release a single tear.

"I feel so cold, like something is wrong with me."

"Nothing is wrong with you," he assured me. "I'm sorry if I made you feel that way. Why do you think you have such a hard time?"

I explained how since I was a kid, my dad would laugh at me whenever I cried. I wasn't ever taken seriously. Some of the stuff I told Josh was stuff I had told over and over again to people who it seemed never cared about my shed tears.

You would think this conversation would've made me more comfortable with the idea of crying, but instead, it made me more resistant and turned off by the idea. My emotions were too uncontrollable, and I needed to feel in control. So, I'd turn to running and my other methods of "safety." This cycle never allowed me to move forward.

My dad was regularly showing up in my dreams, and although I didn't have much knowledge of dreams then, I wholeheartedly believe now dreams are one of the ways God speaks to us, especially me. It's hard to distract yourself with eating disorder behaviors when you're dreaming. I now look back and recognize how persistent He was in talking to me in my dreams and bringing up images to help me process the ache of my soul.

December 10, 2015
I had a dream last night that my dad took me snowmobiling. I miss my dad. I miss him terribly and I hate it. I hate how he wants nothing to do with me and hasn't even called to see how I am. I hate how to be with my dad meant to be without my mom and how now, to be with my mom means to be without

my dad. I wonder why that is; why can't I just have both of my parents a part of my life like a normal person?

Talking to my counselor about all of this has helped, and I'm still trying to become more vulnerable. For so long, I thought I had forgotten how to cry and now think I'm starting to remember. The thought of my dad alone makes me cry, and I just don't know what to do about it. Do I call? Do I text? Do I show up? Write a letter?

Vulnerability is a tough thing. It's a very scary thing, especially when your past experiences being vulnerable haven't been the best. Vulnerability is hard but necessary.

I mentioned to my counselor a few times how much I missed my dad, and after only a few sessions, he proposed an at-home exercise that involved writing a letter to him expressing how I felt.

When I sat down to write, I began to reminisce about old times. It had just turned to winter and the cold was nearing, the same cold months we'd go snowmobiling as a family and stay in the coziness of a cabin and watch the snow while we drank hot cocoa by the fire and ate good food. Although those days were gone, they remained a vivid image in my head.

Dear Dad,
I want you to know I am so thankful for all the things you did for me. We were always going to the coast or camping—to the snow. You've made it clear several times that all you tried to do was be the best dad you could be. I remind myself frequently

of the fun outings we used to have and how much they meant,
and still mean to me.

I wanted my dad to know in my letter the stuff he did didn't go unnoticed. My brother and I both missed him terribly, and I hoped despite our differences, we'd be able to overcome the pain and restore our relationship. I didn't want to keep focusing on the past because I knew it would only further our distance.

If we can both put aside our stubbornness and swallow the
pride rooted from within, I believe we can have a relationship
again; this is something I want and hope you do too.

I've learned through both the turmoil and reconciliation with my dad that holding on to anger is much more difficult than letting go. Regardless of who hurt who, we couldn't take any of it back, and I encouraged my dad to look ahead to the future with me to the things we still had time to change.

I had faith he wanted a relationship with me just as bad as I longed for one with him, and I was willing to do whatever it took to restore what had been broken.

Please consider this letter so that we may reach closure and
start the year off with a new beginning. I don't know if I can get
by with only memories for the rest of my life, and nothing can
or will ever change the fact that you're my dad and I love you.

Josh said I didn't have to send the letter, however, once I allowed myself to process and write out the thoughts and feelings I was carrying, I realized there was a lot I *wanted* to share with my dad. But I was certain I wouldn't receive anything back from him, which was the hardest thing to accept after sending it.

The following week, my counseling appointment went forty minutes overtime. We discussed the letter and created a family tree that listed specific details about each person in my family like addictions they had, childhood wounds they carried, personality traits. The goal of the family tree was to pinpoint patterns that don't excuse but rather explain the behavior of people in your family.

I gained much insight into my dad, and although I didn't know it at the time, that exercise was helping to mend some of the places I still had yet to forgive him.

Shortly after sending the letter, Josh asked what I would want my dad to say if he were to reply. I said I wasn't sure. Everything that came to mind sounded so unlike him, and part of me felt foolish for imagining a world where he might be open to hearing me out and responding with compassion.

"What if you wrote to yourself from your dad's perspective?" he asked.

The idea seemed kind of weird, though. *What is writing a hypothetical letter from my dad supposed to do to help me?*

Despite my doubts, I agreed to it.

The number one thing I begged for from my dad if he were to write back, was empathy.

He would tell me he never knew his drinking would cause me to actually leave, and he didn't understand how unhappy I was. He would understand how the thing I needed from him—more than anything—was his time.

He would remember the moments I pleaded for him to spend quality time with me, to come to one of my sporting events, or to at the *very least* ask me how my day was.

He would notice our differences and recognize how his childhood affected his ability to be there for me in the ways I needed him, how it affected his ability to be there for my mom and brother, too. I wanted him to take ownership of his downfalls and say sorry most of all.

He would acknowledge how quickly I was forced to grow up and how much stress his issues pressed upon me.

He would recall the events I will always hold dear, and the ones he never got to witness because of his stubbornness. He would tell me he's proud of me.

He would reflect on the positive parts of our relationship, forgiving me and deciding he wants a relationship with me.

After completing both of the letters, I brought them into my next counseling session to share with Josh and read them aloud.

"What are you looking for in these letters, Carly?" Josh asked.

I knew much of what I wrote were far-off miracles, but the truth was, I wanted to feel loved.

Deep down, there was this little girl inside of me desperately begging for her father to stretch out his arms and love her unconditionally.

A week or so before the exercise, I had another dream about my dad. This time, we were in the grocery store and he approached me. I can't remember what exactly our conversation entailed, yet I vividly remember him stretching out his arms and welcoming me to find comfort in the warmth of his chest. Although our hug only lasted a brief moment, I latched on tightly, cherishing the hug for as long as I could. It was something I had never felt or experienced with my dad before.

I told Josh that moment was what I hoped to find, something new and undiscovered. *I'd like to think underneath all of the garbage and destruction, there is beauty and hope.*

Eventually, I did find both of those things, but not from my dad.

You Have Everything You Need

Not long after I sent the letter, I received one back. I can't remember what exactly it said, but I do remember it being a different response than the one I had hoped for. However, the fact he wrote back at all was surprising, and from there, we began taking small steps toward full forgiveness as I mentioned earlier.

You see, the new and undiscovered thing I spoke of above came from God. It was acceptance of my earthly father and trust in my heavenly Father. I read the details of that dream now and see the Father I wasn't used to—the one stretching out His arms and welcoming me with warmth and comfort—was God. Once I started putting my trust in Him, the disappointment I faced from my dad was little to none.

It's easier to say this now—being on the other side of the ache—but this took time, and I faced pain and letdown for a while. Still, I continued my journey of healing with my counselor and had a few big, breakthrough moments in the midst of reconnecting with my dad.

March 17, 2016
I never used to think of crying as progress. Before today, I would have thought of crying as a waste of time and energy. All it ever does is put me farther behind. It gets me off schedule. I guess that's why I push aside the way I'm feeling so much. I don't have time to feel sad or afraid. Today when I cried in Josh's office though, he said he saw it as "making progress." I'm sure it's because up until this point, I haven't let my guard down all the way. Every time I get close to that breaking point, I stop myself because I don't want people to know how completely screwed up and fearful I am. But I'm tired of pretending. I'm tired of being alone every night in my room, wishing there was someone there to listen and hear me out. My loneliness and the walls I've been building up have withstood all they can and are finally being torn down. Is it a good thing? Josh seems to think so. I, on the other hand, don't know how I feel about the whole vulnerability thing. The way I look at it right

now is, what do I have to lose? Shoot. It's a Thursday night and I'm sitting in Powell's bookstore eating lentil loops... by myself.

I cry all the time when I am alone—while in the shower, while running, while reading, while thinking of those I love and miss. I'm not embarrassed to cry anymore, but it's still hard for me to allow myself into that place. But by the end of my sessions with Josh, he had seen my red-face, snotty-nosed cry more than once, and I think that was a win in both of our books.

Going to counseling was one of the best decisions I ever made. My counselor helped me confront much of the pain I was suppressing from not having contact with my dad, and by the end of our time together, I looked forward to our sessions.

I couldn't hide anything with him, and even when I tried to change the subject, he'd get quiet and still, waiting for me to answer. I'd have an out-loud dialogue with myself as I tried to understand more of my story.

In the beginning, I'd apologize for how much I talked. To be polite, I'd ask him the same questions he asked me in return, and he'd reply with, "Carly, this session isn't about me."

If you've gone to counseling or therapy, you know the feeling.

What I realize now about my counseling sessions is they weren't something I *had* to go to, they were something I *chose* to go to, mostly because they were free, but also because I knew I couldn't outrun and ignore my problems forever. I made that choice though, not my monsters.

It was time I did something other than write in my journal or talk to someone who didn't have the skills to help, and it was time I talked to a professional whose job it was to listen and ask the right questions. That's really what it was. Josh asked the best questions, which always led *me* to find the answers.

He never answered anything for me. He never prescribed medication. And even when I asked him, "What do you think?" he would tell me it didn't matter. He showed me how all of the things I was searching for outside of myself were instead accessible inside of myself.

Overcoming the Stuff that Gets in the Way

Sometimes I think who we are gets lost in the worrying of who others are.

Wow, that person is so talented!
That could never be me.

What I'm starting to find is much of the tools, confidence, and spark we need to start our engines and lead us toward the path of healing and success (however you define success) are all within us. Sometimes deep, deep down, but they are there.

I'm not saying the way to find them is by ourselves (although much of our hyper-individualistic world would probably disagree), but I am saying through Jesus and with community, we do have the potential to grow out of our hand-me-downs and into our wedding gowns.

Sometimes we hit a wall before making it to the stage, but it's through persistence, vulnerability, and faith we can and will see a better day and a better us.

My eating disorder demanded a lot from me, one demand being to live a life of secrecy. My monsters let me know if I told anyone, I'd lose everything. I'd be even more worthless and alone.

In Brené Brown's book *The Gifts of Imperfection*, she discusses how shame grows in our lives and what we must do to stop it from growing.

> Shame needs three things to grow out of control in our lives: secrecy, silence, and judgment. When something shaming happens and we keep it locked up, it festers and grows. It consumes us. We need to share our experience. Shame happens between people, and it heals between people. If we find someone who has earned the right to hear our story, we need to tell it. Shame loses power when it is spoken. In this way, we need to cultivate our story to let go of shame, and we need to develop shame resilience in order to cultivate our story.[46]

Through practicing shame resilience, Brené says we will find more courage, compassion, and connection. But we only get there by talking about "the things that get in the way."

---

46 Brown, *The Gifts of Imperfection*, 40.

The shame.
The fear.
The vulnerability.
The hard stuff.

One of the things to help me most during my recovery was hearing the stories of other women who had dealt with an eating disorder similar to mine. I started listening to a podcast called *Recovery Warriors* while studying abroad in Australia and vividly remember more than once being in the kitchen making food, or being out for a run, and breaking down in tears.

To hear someone share their story and specifically highlight moments or memories I thought I was alone in was such a healing, refreshing, and freeing experience. I couldn't stop listening, and I couldn't believe I had lived so long believing I was alone.

I still had a ways to go before this breakthrough moment after wrapping up my counseling sessions and freshman year of college, but I was slowly inching my way forward, and that's what is important.

There's truly so much beauty we encounter through storytelling. One of the biggest reasons I chose to write this book was because of how drastically I've been impacted and changed by other people's stories.

As I continue, it is my hope you, too, walk away feeling a little less alone and a little more comforted. Nobody can do the hard work it takes to change for you, but knowing others have walked a similar path will certainly make your journey easier.

CHAPTER 14

MOVING OUT OF THE CORNER AND INTO COMMUNITY

———

I don't want to worship running in an unhealthy way, but sometimes running is the only thing I know how to do when I don't know how to do anything else.

The one thing I've learned throughout my journey is you cannot recover alone.

Navigating something as difficult and heavy as recovery from an addiction requires community. Without it, you are likely to fall into a pit of loneliness, inhibiting you from moving forward.

I've had many toilsome moments when loneliness swallowed me alive, moments when all I wanted to do was numb myself because it seemed easier to turn to distractions promising peace than bear the difficult work it takes to heal.

Even after such an eye-opening experience like the one in my Family Communication class, I wasn't ready to accept I had an eating disorder and wanted to brush it off as no big deal.

I was just being emotional.

I had completed the first steps of recovery: noticing the problem, thinking about what I might do to change, and wanting to change. But when recovery begged more from me, it was too much and too hard on my own.

I couldn't say goodbye to my addiction just yet because I had no idea what life would look like if I did. *What would I look like?*

My denial and distraction are what ultimately caused me to label 2016 as a lost year. It was a year when I clung tightly to my eating disorder behaviors because I was afraid to let them go, a year when I sought attention from men because I thought I might find comfort and acceptance, a year when I wanted more of God, but not if it meant giving Him more of me, and a year I was let down after realizing the things I was putting my trust in were fleeting.

I'm just going to say it: life is a process. Life is a long, drawn-out, sometimes very frustrating process. And to give up on the process is tempting when all around us we have distractions that are often easy, quick to come by, and don't make us approach the deep, dark parts of us that need healing.

You see, it wasn't until a few years into my discipleship to Jesus I started to appreciate the painful places I sometimes find myself wandering back through. I've come to realize it's in those moments—the moments when we remember how broken or scared we were in our lives—God wants to bring forth healing and restoration.

It's never His will to bring about hardship, and oftentimes when all we can focus on is the negative in our lives, it's because we haven't slowed down long enough to quiet ourselves and listen for what He wants to do in that season or situation.

God's will is to deliver us from our hardship. Only in trusting and believing in His sovereign truth will we reach complete victory and triumph over our brokenness.

Other things in life will try to convince us they have the same authority as God. Some are more subtle than others, yet most of us know the places we put our hope during rough times in our life aren't always beneficial. Still, we ruthlessly grab on to such distractions, unable to let go because we fear if we did, we would be left with nothing.

We cling to what is tangible when we've never experienced the intangible. Put another way, we grab the next drink, type the next Google search, scroll through feed after feed, meet up with stranger after stranger, and busy ourselves into oblivion when we've never let Jesus walk us through our garden of ashes.

Each time I've chosen to follow after the fleeting promises of this world, I'm reminded of these words spoken by Jesus in the book of Matthew:

Enter by the narrow gate. For the gate is wide and the way is easy that leads to destruction, and those who enter by it are many. For the gate is narrow and the way is hard that leads to life, and those who find it are few.[47]

In this chapter, I want to show you the distractions I've turned to time and time again, and the failure I've encountered from them over and over. My hope is through my vulnerability you will find strength in your process and turn to both Jesus and community for the help you need moving forward.

My hope also is you will not give up the process when you meet obstacles, and instead of choosing Jesus and community, choose numbing activities to cope. Life is a process because it's not perfect, and shame won't get you anywhere except for farther away from the person you're meant to be.

Whatever You Do, Don't Stop Running

Toward the end of my freshman year of college, I started seeing a physical therapist due to excruciating pain I was experiencing in both of my knees from running.

After my first appointment, my physical therapist told me I had poor form and low muscle mass, and if I wanted to see improvement, I needed to take down my mileage and work toward strengthening other parts of my body.

---

47   Matt. 7:13-14 (ESV).

She didn't get it. *Take down my mileage?* My monsters wouldn't let me do such a thing. There were no days off.

But in time (and I mean a lot of time) I decided to listen to my physical therapist, but there were conditions. There always were. I'd lower my runs to three miles and wouldn't go past fifteen a week. On the days I didn't run, I'd ride the stationary bike or swim laps in the pool. I would do exercises given to me by my physical therapist but not as my only source of exercise. I'd do them before or after my "official workout," which was never less than an hour and a half long.

I'd keep a log of all these things to make sure I never stepped out of line.

After I ate "bad," my time in the gym would increase. Some mornings I would run to physical therapy because I didn't understand the concept of rest. I wanted to feel better, yet not if that meant gaining weight or losing all the "progress" I had made.

I truly believed without running I wouldn't be the same person. I hadn't taken a break since high school, and the thought of having something I loved so much taken away from me was unbearable. Most days, I found sore knees worth not having to deal with the shame that came from not running to compensate for everything I ate.

I would run, even if it meant having to walk super slow on the stairs to and from class, constantly adjusting or rubbing my knees from irritation and throbbing, and lying to my friends about my pain whenever they asked how I was feeling.

Finally, I decided to listen to my physical therapist completely. I didn't have a choice. I had to stop all exercise involving my legs or else I would, without a doubt, be in a wheelchair.

I still went to the gym every day and would do workout routines to strengthen my core, arms, and shoulders. After we tweaked my running form for a couple of months and I gained some strength, I was discharged and cleared to return to *minimal* running.

Only, I didn't quite listen to the "minimal" part.

I started to reach new heights in my running and got so excited by the improvement I was seeing, I decided to sign up for my first half marathon.

One Monday I ran ten miles, and the next I ran eleven miles even faster. I journaled right after this and wrote, *I feel super in control.*

I ran my half marathon successfully at the end of that summer, but somewhere between the asphalt and my sneakers, I upset my knees again and ended up in physical therapy a second time.

Not being able to run always made me feel depressed, hyperaware of what I was eating, and angry. Both times I saw a physical therapist, I couldn't let it go until my body flat out said, "No more!"

October 21, 2016

It's been one week and five days since I've run. Only five days if you count last Sunday when I went out and ran three miles because I was too stubborn not to. It only made matters worse. I wish my happiness didn't depend so heavily on running, but I can't help it. It does something to me and without it, I feel empty and incomplete. I know it sounds depressing but it's true. I've been so negative and unpleasant to be around.

It's no wonder to me now why a lack of running produced an abundance of uncomfortable feelings.

I was searching for something, and because I never allowed myself to slow down, I wasn't able to identify what that something was. I was running from those dang monsters and running from stillness because I feared the quiet. Little did I know it's the stillness and quiet where we discover so many of the answers we've been looking for.

Searching for Something

Amid my physical therapy epidemic, I finished my freshman year of college, moved into my first studio apartment, and started working at a cafe only a block down the road after enrolling in summer classes. All of my friends returned home for the summer but returning home wasn't an option for me. My mom was in the middle of packing herself and my siblings up to move across the state to Baker City, Oregon, where my grandparents had moved a short time before, and I didn't exactly have a place to call home.

Still, I was okay with staying in Portland for the summer. I'd make new friends. Maybe I'd even meet a boy and fall in love. The opportunities were endless, I thought.

What I enjoyed most about living alone was not having to rely on anyone else and getting to decide for myself what I wanted to do each day, what I wanted to eat, and who I wanted to see. I loved being able to come home knowing everything was still in its place, and I loved that nothing interfered with my plans. It sounds selfish because it was. And it sounds like I was content, but I wasn't.

Take the below journal entry for instance. At first glance, it would seem as if I was perfectly okay, yet what you don't see is the low-grade anxiety I carried with me daily while doing activities like the ones listed.

Learning to Live Alone:
Wake up
Go to the gym
Take a bath
Make a smoothie naked
Make coffee too
Sing out loud
Go to piano lessons (and then shopping!)
Eat leftover takeout (Thai curry)
Sit in the park blocks and write for three hours
Go for a run and watch the sun go down
Dance to girly songs while you make dinner
Drink wine
Sleep Merrily my darling

I was living in a world of my own making while doing everything in my power to convince myself I was happy. I was letting fear determine what I'd do each day because I was afraid to do anything outside of my comfort zone. When I'd feel guilty for not doing more or for not being "enough," I'd take myself on dates, eat the sweet and salty things I felt undeserving of, and seek after men.

I downloaded two dating apps that summer and spent most nights swiping through hundreds of profiles and rapidly searching for someone to give me a source of fulfillment.

I can be daring. I can do things alone. I can serial date and not get attached to anyone.

I'd read my Bible or devotional every morning and would pray to God. That was my "Jesus time" for the day, and after those fifteen or thirty minutes, I would go on worrying, doubting, judging, and worshipping things that only brought more trouble into my life.

I had tried my freshman year of college to just be me. It turned out people didn't like the real version of me. At least that's what my monsters told me.

You wear weird clothes. You spend a lot of time doing weird things, like cooking dinner or reading in your dorm room on Friday nights.

You rarely sleep in. You spend the mornings praying, and you study more than you hang out with your friends.

The one thing I actually did hear people say about me is I was *that tall girl*.

"You know, that tall blonde who is always running."

So, after trying on the shoe of originality and having it "fail," I decided I'd try doing what all the other girls getting attention were doing. *I do need to loosen up. I do need to have more fun. I am too serious. I am too set in my ways.*

Soon after this realization, I was laying in the grass on my school campus one afternoon, and there was a group of girls on a blanket near me discussing when their fake IDs would be arriving. As they talked amongst each other, I began to imagine the rest of summer and how much better it would be if only I had a fake ID, too.

I love music. I could see all my favorite singers and songwriters in Portland at all the cool venues that are twenty-one and older. I could buy wine at the grocery store and spend summer nights drinking a nice red blend and reflecting in my apartment.

These were the two biggest reasons I told myself I wanted to get a fake ID at age nineteen, yet if I'm being completely honest, the real reason I wanted one was so I could go out to bars with men I met online and hopefully—just hopefully—meet the man of my dreams. *Or, maybe I could be that girl who shows up to the bar alone and gets approached by a handsome guy who makes me want to be spontaneous, forget all my responsibility, and wander around Portland for the night.*

Before I had time to be rational with myself, I was already induced by the idea.

"Hey, did I hear you guys say something about fake IDs?"

Where Is the Freedom?

At first, living alone was everything I wanted—independence, cleanliness, quietness. Only when summer turned into a much different experience than what I expected was I upset with my choice to stay in Portland.

I didn't make friends or meet the boyfriend I dreamt I would. I did meet a lot of people and go on a lot of dates, yet most nights ended the same: lonely. I encountered a loneliness so deep, I forgot there were people in my life who loved and cared about me.

Outside of my church community who I met with every Tuesday, I didn't have many people to talk to. I was working almost every day of the week and had classes two days a week. I still didn't have a car and couldn't exactly explore the city in the ways I wished I could.

For this reason, living in my studio apartment only comforted my monsters more, and before I knew it I had adopted a whole new edition to my eating disorder.

You see, shame likes to keep us in a corner. When there is nobody there to interfere with the lies we're believing, that's when shame does its best work.

Because of this, I continued to ignore my eating disorder, pretending the realization in my communications class never happened. The more time passed, the crazier I sounded to myself.

If I truly had an eating disorder, then where was my mom to help me? What about my dad? And my friends? Both of my parents were absent and too busy with their own lives, it seemed, and all my friends left.

Who cares if I like to run and eat healthy? There's nothing wrong with that.
These are the things that bring me happiness.
If I did have an eating disorder, I'm better now.
I gained some weight, I gained some muscle.

I soon developed a love for cooking and would experiment often. Only, I hated the feeling of sitting down alone to enjoy the meal I worked so hard on. On the flip side, I didn't like eating with other people because I felt judged. I ate more than my friends because of how restricted my diet was, and when I felt out of control, I wanted to be able to overeat in peace.

Eventually, I got the idea to start an Instagram titled "Carly's Counter," where I would share pictures of my food to inspire other people to eat healthier. I found my page to be a creative outlet and a way for me to explore my passion for health and fitness more deeply while connecting with those who had similar passions.

Shortly after, I started following a few accounts that told me when I should be eating, what I should be eating, and how much I should be eating. I listened to these people because they had thousands of followers, and I interpreted their love for kale as a license of authority to educate people on their nutrition.

However, Ragen Chastain, a National Eating Disorders Association ambassador, says these external rules are a dangerous aspect of diet culture and should be resisted. "Food has plenty of appropriate uses in our culture, including nourishment, celebration, and emotional eating, but trying to manipulate our body size is not one of them."[48]

But because I wanted to be fit like these women, I'd adopt their food rules and spend entire evenings researching workouts and coming up with strict plans so I wouldn't embarrass myself in the gym. I became obsessed with "clean eating" and building lean muscle and thought, *If my knees aren't going to allow me to run, I'll fall in love with weightlifting.*

I fantasized about being toned and shiny like a photoshopped supermodel and told myself, *As long as I eat clean food, it doesn't matter how much I eat!*

I look back and see "clean eating" (a term I despise now) as an attempt to tune into my love for cooking while still maintaining the fitness and body goals I sought. Because that's what all the "experts" said you had to do. There was no room for "empty calories" if you wanted a six-pack.

---

48 Ragen Chastain, "Recognizing and Resisting Diet Culture," *National Eating Disorder Association* (blog), September 13, 2020.

Even under the false messaging I fell for, there was a deeper story taking place: food never left me, and everyone else had. It brought comfort to my loneliness but not for long.

July 8, 2016
Living alone is such a pleasure at times, but it can make you feel crazy. Lately, I've felt insane. I'm starting to understand that's what happens when you go to bed alone, wake up alone, and DO EVERYTHING ALONE. Thank goodness for wine though... and chocolate... and clean sheets. I have all three of those things tonight and it's a refreshing feeling. I wonder though, is all of this worth it? Are good wine and a clean studio apartment worth all of the loneliness I feel?

Some nights, my monsters were so loud and my thoughts so dark, they scared me.

August 3, 2016
There is something wrong with me.
Something deeply wrong with me.
I am twisted,
Deceitful,
Selfish,
And lonely.
This is how I've felt lately.
I've felt careless.
I've felt like everything I do has been done with half as much effort. Yet, I don't care.
I've felt weak and exhausted. Both physically and mentally.
I've felt stupid and fat... unhealthy and useless.
Every time I bathe, it's like I'm trying to cleanse myself from the dirt and grime encompassing my every move.

At work, I feel insignificant and judged.
I know God has a greater plan than how I'm feeling now. I know He loves me as His daughter and has already washed me white as snow, but I'm still uncertain of this truth. I'm not sure if my unbelief is a result of my lack of faith or my lack of motivation. I'm just going through the motions.

I'd stay up late in a state of anxiousness and torment, driving myself crazy. I became engulfed by the fact I was lonely and convinced myself that's how it always would be.

Still, all I wished for was to be okay with my circumstances and to love myself fully. On one of my late nights, I wrote a poem about my current state.

July 7, 2016... just after midnight
The world sees her standing tall
They tell her she has a beautiful smile
To never settle for less than she deserves
She feels she deserves nothing
She feels she doesn't feel
She is emotionless
Always anxious
Lonely
Everyone close to her, she has shut the door on.
She thinks of herself as "out of touch" but lacks the knowledge on how to be more in touch
She wants love
A happy life
Time to herself
Time with others
Time

The truth is, I was miserable. I didn't like the path I was on. I wanted to see God in my problems but was blind to His presence because I was caught up in my world too small for hope and full of distraction.

I wanted to get out of the rut I was in but didn't know how. I was waking up regularly to anxiety attacks where I was so wrapped up in my thoughts, I'd pace around my apartment because I didn't know where to start or what to do first each day. I'd endlessly procrastinate and worry to the point where tasks that should only take a few minutes would take me twenty or thirty.

I see now I was looking to fill a void only God can fill, and I kept failing. Staring back at my reflection, I wondered how many more times I'd find myself in this repetitive cycle of disappointment and angst.

My need to be "good" and to "do things right" had a crippling effect that left me without words. The thought of praying weighed me down and felt like more of a chore than it did anything else. I'd write about how big of a failure and hypocrite I was for running to God for forgiveness over and over.

I was tired of always feeling like I needed something or someone to make me happy.

August 6, 2016
It's like the only thing I care about lately is my body and looking sexy. My morals are slowly leaving my side, I'm questioning my purpose more often than not, and I feel lost. I don't know how I got here, and I don't know how to get out. I don't know

if I even want out at the moment. I don't know what I want. I thought there was freedom in the unknown, but I don't feel free.

I would experience moments of freedom... but not for long. What did the most damage was not inviting anyone into my darkness. This is what ultimately caused me to react so dramatically to everything around me. It invaded my sense of faith.

No date
I am in a rut—I am down. So far in, lost and lonely... I don't know what to do. I cover up my pain, anxiousness, nervousness, and fear with money, sex (not actual sex... but close enough), MATERIAL THINGS, DISTRACTIONS, IDOLS, busyness, food, exercise, etc., etc., etc., etc., etc., etc. My head feels heavy, crowded, and cloudy. I can't grasp my thoughts or make anything out clearly. I can't just be in one moment at a time. Instead, I am in so many moments—so many at just one time. I've drifted so far from my faith... from God. Tonight, I saw my pastor in Powell's and had the perfect opportunity to talk to him but didn't. I got so embarrassed and felt stupid. I felt like a hypocrite to, on a Sunday, go up and introduce myself to the pastor who just got done with the church service I never attended. I felt like he knew. Everyone knows that I'm a hypocrite, lost and afraid. Everyone knows I'm pretending to be someone I'm not.

I didn't know it at the time, but I was *so* angry. I was running circles, unsure of my purpose, and unaware of how to find a new route. My identity was warped by lies I'd try to cover up with a different mask every day, hoping just one of them would work.

Life appeared easy for those around me, and I'd get exhausted from caring as much as I did about who I was and how I was living. I wanted to escape it all. I wanted to care less. I wanted to not feel shame. I wanted to do the things other college students were doing.

I partied last night. Went to a festival on the waterfront, got kicked out when they discovered my fake ID was indeed fake, drank more when I got home, smoked some weed at a friend's, went downtown to some Thai restaurant supposed to be having a dance party, and then left early to go get Mediterranean food from the food carts. I made friends with one of the guys working, ate a huge lamb shawarma—drunk on the curb—and I can't even remember if I liked it.

That night, my monsters left me alone. For once, they didn't criticize how I was acting or what I was doing. I felt relieved, even if it meant pretending to be someone I wasn't and waking up with a hangover the next day. *At least they were quiet.*

The truth is, I wanted to belong. I wanted love, and I wanted peace more than anything. I still want these things, yet at that time in my life, I mistakenly believed a relationship was the only way to attain them.

I had a friend say to me recently, "Carly, you're so aware and mindful, always trying to improve yourself and the world around you. You know what is right from wrong and it seems every area of your life is in sync, except when it comes to relationships."

This is a friend who knows me so well, it disgusts me. But she was right, and I told her she was right. I've always struggled to mature out of old habits exemplified by my family and pressed into me over time.

More than once, my lips have said "yes" to what I've heard from God, while my actions have pushed back with a hard "no" and a stand of resistance. Going against what God says will lead to True life and deciding for myself how I will live.

Why does this keep happening?

I had full confidence in all Jesus had done in my life up until this point. The rough patches He'd turned into smooth roads and the broken pieces He'd made into art. Yet the mantra, "Do what makes you happy," rung so loudly choosing a different way felt impossible.

I've always known right from wrong, but like most humans, I often find myself doing things I know aren't in my best interest because somewhere in the mix comes desire. Desire is so strong it often invades and overtakes the very thing we are after. That is, love and belonging. And not love and belonging from another human but from God. Nothing beats love and belonging from Him.

I'm slowly learning the pressure we face from society is a free pass that comes at a nasty price when we choose what feels good over what proves good. What many of us (including me) forget is the instant gratification we find in other things and other people is not always here to stay.

Shame Doesn't Have the Final Say

2016 was full of adventures I thought were necessary to achieve happiness. Parties, drinking, planning my days around men who—as we can see—are no longer in the picture. At times, these things felt essential to my overall health... the cure to my anxiety; fitting in and feeling admired. And although both drinking and dating can be two very healthy things, I don't think the way I used them in 2016 was.

My goal for 2017 (upon many others) is to not take shortcuts... I want what I do to count. I want to face my emotions full-on and approach them with the confidence that, despite the way I may be feeling, God's got my back and His love is never changing. I want to, whenever I feel lost, know that He's not going to lead me astray if I cling to His truth, love, justice, grace, and mercy.

Shortly before writing this journal entry, it became apparent why I was struggling so much. I was missing a key ingredient: Jesus. I couldn't see past all the negative gunk in my life because it was *all* I was focusing on. Until I had success in my relationship with Him, I was going to continue facing failed relationships, loneliness, and anxiety.

Classifying 2016 as a year when I was blind is the best way I see fit to express the beautiful life kept hidden from me. I had so many things to be grateful for, only the gifts I'd been given were corroded with doubt and a false identity. They were there all along, and every once in awhile, I'd start to recognize this for myself.

The same year, Corey Ciocchetti—college professor, motivational speaker, and author—asked me and a room full of other college students the four questions below. I thoughtfully responded to each one.

Who am I?
I am independent. I am strong. I am insecure and worry too much about what other people think of me. I am smart.

Where am I going?
I don't know where I'm going, and I guess that's where a lot of my anxiety comes from—from not knowing. I get overwhelmed with so many possibilities of where to go. I thought I knew what I wanted, and I thought I had a plan. Now, I have nothing. What do you do when the plan you thought you would follow doesn't work out?

How am I going to get there?
Right now, my goal is to have some sort of direction on where to go. I'm going to get there by first figuring out what makes me happy and how to be happy. I need to set my priorities straight and make sure they're in alignment with my heart.

Who am I taking with me?
I'm taking this road all on my own. I have no one. No boyfriend. No friends. Of course, I have family, but I think these next couple of years I need to focus on me.

If I were to rewrite my responses to the questions above, I would certainly have more to say. Not because I know all the answers, but because I trust in a God who provides me with a roadmap that allows for adventure and spontaneity.

I'd also replace the word "happy" with joyful because I've learned the difference between the two and don't just want a temporary feeling based on external inputs around me. Instead, I want a deep feeling of contentment. One that comes from within and sticks around through all of the highs and lows of life. Becoming more in touch with joy means becoming less influenced by momentary bits of happiness, and I want that feeling.

The last thing I would change is this statement: *I'm taking this road all on my own. I have no one.* That's a complete lie from the enemy and one I had yet to realize. No, I didn't have a boyfriend or many friends at the time, but I did have a church community and friends outside of Portland. I also had, and always have had, Jesus.

The problem wasn't that I didn't have anyone; the problem was I didn't trust anyone aside from myself. I didn't let anyone into my gunk, which is why I ended up on a lonely road where many of the caring and loving faces around me disappeared.

It was too foggy for me to see the light in my life and even when I tried, I always came to the solution I needed to do things on my own, the exact opposite of how Jesus asks us to live.

Jesus knew we would be tempted by the ways of the world, and there would be many times when we decided to trust ourselves and how we feel more than we trust Him. But I've learned over the last few years relying solely on how I feel won't ever move me toward a fuller or more joyful life.

I now understand in a new way what He meant when He said to find our life; we have to first lose it.[49] We have to let go of how we feel and trust in what He says because sometimes our "feelers" are off.

He told us many people would choose the wide gate, the way that's easy and leads to destruction.[50] I think a big part of what he meant was many people would try to decide for themselves how to live, and a big part of their decisions would be based on their feelings.

He then said only a few people would choose the narrow gate, the way that's hard and leads to life, which I now believe was Him driving home the point only a few people would learn to go against their "feelers" and trust His word.[51] And man, I want to be one of those few people. I always have, but *it is hard* and takes so much sacrifice.

The world will shout lessons of self-love and self-acceptance, both of which are important. Even more important, however, is recognizing the love and acceptance we've already been given in Christ.

There will be many days when loving and accepting ourselves presents challenge after challenge. But if we can get to a place where we believe deep in our bones, spirit, soul, and mind we're already—without fail and without falter—loved,

---

49 Matt. 10:39 (ESV).
50 Matt. 7:13 (ESV).
51 Matt. 7:14 (ESV).

admired, cherished, and accepted by Jesus, then nothing and nobody can take that away from us.

I was so far from this place at age nineteen, and because I relied so much on myself, I often faced exhaustion and a sudden prompting to get up and run away from it all.

For this reason, the first year I lived alone was both a positive and negative experience. Positive in the way it taught me to laugh at myself, be comfortable with the uncomfortable, practice silence and solitude, and get more creative with my cooking. But negative in the ways it influenced me to hide, dwell on the past, manipulate and plan each day perfectly, and give into lustful behaviors.

I've found when we try to decide for ourselves what we need and listen to our monsters, the result is anxiety, depression, aimlessness, and exhaustion. In comparison, when we allow God into our decisions, the result is life, love, purpose, and beauty; the result is wholeness.

When I started to find company in good friends and God instead of distraction, I began to experience more of the freedom I was after. This doesn't mean I didn't revert into my humanness at times (heck, I still do!), but inch by inch, I was moving forward.

Closing this chapter of my life felt like closing the door to a very confusing time which, to this day, I find myself puzzled over. But I think that's okay.

If life were static, there wouldn't be much to learn or experience. We'd know it all, do it all, and have it all.

You will have seasons of sadness, frustration, and loneliness, but you will most certainly experience more positive seasons as well.

To keep your hope engaged in the not-so-positive seasons, you cannot let shame have the final say.

My prayer for you today is to not ever be taken captive by the lie that you are alone.

Shadows and darkness may linger, but your cry does not go left unheard. If you ever start to doubt this truth, read this prayer aloud:

God,
Help me to see myself the way You do. Remove the lie that I'm
unlovable and alone and replace it with the truth I'm accepted
and heard. Give me the courage to share my pain with a loving
community placed in my life by You and meet me in the places
of need I'm unable to name myself. I thank You for Your grace
when I fall short of who You've created me to be and trust that
You're more than a momentary feeling. In Jesus' name, Amen.

CHAPTER 15

BREAKING FREE

_____

A wise person once told me,

"*I don't think it's smart to approach life with an impoverished mindset because you limit yourself from new and unexpected things that may enter your life at any moment. That's what I'm learning life is more about, the joy that comes from the unexpected.*"

I began writing this book after living in Australia for six months and having the time of my life. My decision to leave the country was partially spontaneous and partially planned. I knew when I started college on a scholarship through the Ford Family Foundation I wanted to take advantage of the opportunity to study abroad. My scholarship foundation was willing to help with the cost, and I had heard too many positive experiences not to consider it.

Soon after the new year in 2017, I finalized my decision to study at James Cook University in Cairns, Australia, and prepared for my first trip outside of the country.

I couldn't imagine what being in Australia would be like until the plane landed and I stepped outside into the hot air. Immersed in slang terms I found funny and birds I found beautiful, I needed to get away from my mess to realize I was indeed in a mess; I was relying too much on myself and too little on God.

Being in Cairns felt like a dream, unlike anything I had ever experienced. It was unreal living next to a line of beaches, waking up to sunshine and warm air every day (even in December!), riding my bike to uni and being able to hop in the car and within minutes be in the Daintree Rainforest or at the loading dock to head out to the Great Barrier Reef.

Each day, I woke up wondering how I got so lucky. *Why me?*

What I didn't know at the start of 2017 was it was going to be a very big year for me full of adventure, learning, laughter, and growth. It would be both challenging and joyous, and I would learn more about others, myself, and Jesus.

Learning to Trust My Intuition

I've learned through my own story and education that eating disorders don't leave much room for spontaneity. Most victims have a structured idea of when they will eat each day, what they will eat, who they will eat with, and how they will get rid of the food after. That is, if they choose to eat at all.

You've probably noticed throughout my story I rarely left room for spontaneity, and whenever I did, I felt anxious.

After finalizing my decision to go to Australia, I started to take my recovery more seriously because I knew obsessing over food and my body would ruin my time abroad. The eating and exercise routines I had were sure to strip my experience of all spontaneity, and I couldn't let that happen.

There's nothing wrong with being a person who likes or craves routine, but routine never allowed me to overcome my fears. When I started making room for the unexpected, I began to appreciate more than the nutritional value of food.

One of the ways I did this was by working to accept when something interfered with my meal plans. I'd still keep a rough idea in my head of the foods I'd like to eat each day, but if something else came up, I tried not to view it as the end of the world.

I stopped studying every restaurant's website before going out to eat with friends or family, and I took it as a challenge each time I was handed a menu by a waitress.

How long will it take me to decide?
Can I be present for the conversation and still enjoy the food I chose without being preoccupied with my decision?
What can I focus on instead of my caloric intake and exercise punishment afterward?

Eating unplanned meals or snacks outside of my "safe" zone was terrifying at first. I'd go out to eat with a friend while trying to listen to what they were saying, and my monsters wouldn't shut up.

You shouldn't have ordered that.
They probably added so much oil.
You're for sure gaining weight from this meal.
Why didn't you just do the safe thing and order a salad?
Now you have to run even more tomorrow.

I'd feel judged for being indecisive and ordering things typically deemed "unhealthy." I'd wonder how my friends were able to be so attentive to the conversation when the only thing I could focus on was the food. I started to think about how the challenge I set for myself wasn't as good of an idea as I initially thought. I'd feel paralyzed.

However, every once in awhile, I'd have a breakthrough moment that made me feel empowered by my choice, and when those moments happened, I was overcoming a food fear. Going after what I wanted, not what my monsters told me I had to have to maintain my image, I started to realize standing strong in my decisions is what quieted my monsters. I couldn't let them continue to push me around.

To overcome any fear, you must have a reason, and my reason was to recover.

But I failed more than I succeeded because it's hard to forget the rules you've lived by for so long.

In her memoir, *Everything I Know About Love,* Dolly Alderton puts it this way:

You can restore your physical being to health; you can develop a rational, balanced, caring attitude to weight as well as good daily habits. But you can't forget how many calories are in a boiled egg or how many steps burn how many calories. You can't forget what exact weight you were every month that made up that time. You can try as hard as you can to block it out, but sometimes, on very difficult days, it feels like you'll never be as euphoric as that ten-year-old licking lurid jam off her fingertips, not ever again.[52]

Just as I wasn't able to imagine what living in Australia would be like until I was there, I wasn't able to imagine what life recovered would be like until I was out of my disordered way of living, forced to live a new kind of life.

If you've ever traveled or been to a foreign place, then you know it's hard to worry too much about the food you consume when there are so many other things begging for your attention and time. Because of this, I found my first steps to recovery much more accessible.

I was experiencing so many changes, and whenever I did have the urge to revert to old ways, I'd slow down and ask myself why I came to Australia. Interestingly enough, each time I asked myself that question, food or exercise never came up.

Right before leaving for my sixth-month excursion, I began learning a lot about intuitive eating and hoped I could

---

52 Dolly Alderton, *Everything I Know About Love: A Memoir* (New York: HarperCollins, 2020), 77.

practice it more while abroad. Intuitive eating is about breaking free from diet culture, tuning into the hunger you're experiencing, and being able to satisfy that hunger guilt-free while enjoying each food experience for what it is.

It involves getting curious and letting that curiosity lead you to trust your body more and more as you move closer to food freedom. No foods are off-limits when you're living an intuitive eating lifestyle, yet that doesn't mean it's a free-for-all to binge or overindulge. However, when you do binge or overindulge, intuitive eating still begs for your acceptance, knowing the food experience alone does not define you.

There were plenty of times where I thought the whole intuitive eating thing wasn't for me.

All it's going to do is set me up to gain a ton of weight and constantly be in a state of panic!

Any time I did start to make some headway, my monsters always crept back in.

You're blowing up.
You better work out twice as hard today to make up for that cake last night.
If you think you can just eat whatever you want and still stay thin, you're wrong.

It's no wonder I had thoughts like this. You see, when you move from a place of intense restriction, obsession, and fear of food to a place of allowance, acceptance, and approval, it's hard to know just when you are full or hungry. It's even harder to disable the shame trigger that gets released after a particular food experience.

Meaning, there were many days where I still restricted my food intake and obsessed over a meal or food choice I made while trying with all my might to *just accept it* and to accept myself.

What made my intuitive eating journey more obtainable was eating with other people who were eating intuitively, too, whether they knew it or not. My monsters couldn't corner me as easily when I wasn't the only one eating the cake or grabbing seconds.

Granted, I still had to deal with the noisy inner dialogue when I ate with others, yet not feeling so alone in my cravings gave me permission to ignore that dialogue and remind myself I am not cut off from the sweet and salty things in life as I once believed before.

If they can order pasta and still give me the attention I deserve, I can do the same.
These monsters don't get to control me anymore.

Finding Family in a Foreign Place

I decided to live with a host family while in Australia because I imagined in doing so, I wouldn't be able to stress about food and my body as much. I'd have to eat whatever was put in front of me, being thankful for the people willing to open their home up to me. In addition, I thought it would immerse me in Australian culture more and give me a source of community.

I had heard from other people who lived with host families and loved it. However, because of unforeseen circumstances, my stay didn't last long. After a week of living with them, I found out:

1. My host mom didn't like to cook and wasn't a great cook.
2. They were only home for a couple of hours each night and usually got home when I was about to take off to hang out with friends.
3. They decided to get a divorce shortly before I arrived.

In addition to these three things, I was living in a granny flat apart from the family's house. It felt no different than living alone in my studio back in Portland, which was my red flag.

When I got the flu early on in my stay and was stuck in the flat for close to five days, I decided my host family probably wasn't the best fit for me. So, after a week of being sick, I talked to my host mom, and we agreed finding another place to stay would be a wise move for both of us.

In no time, I began renting out a room in a house that had three other male students living in it. I hadn't ever lived with all guys but only had a week to find another place to live and was pretty much hooked when I found out they had an organized task list for cleaning every week. It was by far the nicest house I've ever lived in; there was an in-ground swimming pool, ping pong table, gym, and a huge kitchen.

Each week, two of my housemates and I would go grocery shopping together (a nightmare for me but another challenge I accepted). They had an entire menu planned out for days ahead. We had fajitas one day, curry, sushi, stir fry, or burgers the others, and crepes on the weekends.

From the very start of being there, they invited me to join in on their partnered cooking. I was hesitant to join in on every meal—especially without being in control of the ingredients we used—yet I did agree to a couple each week.

Eating with two big men who paid no attention to caloric (or shall I say, kilojoule) intake and the health content of food shifted my perspective on food. There was never any judgment at the table, and I learned to let go of some of the minuscule worries I let interfere with enjoying what I was eating.

Some nights I'd be in my room studying and I'd get a knock on the door telling me to come out to eat some pie or to try a cookie they had just made. We'd get in the car after grocery shopping and one of them would chuck a candy bar into the back seat because "They were on sale and they're our favorite!"

My roommates were constantly telling me how healthy I ate, and even though I knew, hearing it from other people was both a reminder and reason for me to let loose.

Shortly after moving in with the guys, I started working at a cafe down the road and met one of my good friends, Astrid. We'd go swimming after work, grab a beer from time to time, and hang out with her mom, June.

Astrid showed me all of the best hiking and hang-out spots in Cairns. She had spent her whole life there and took me under her wing in more ways than one.

I eventually moved in with Astrid, June, her younger brother, and their dog Sancho. They had a spare bedroom and the price was way more affordable than the fancy house I was living in at the time, so I packed my bags and set up my third bedroom in Cairns.

I soon realized being with Astrid and June was exactly what I wanted when I signed up to be paired with a host family. They were everything I'd asked for and more. I had a constant sense during my three months there that God was at work in all of us.

Right before moving in, June and her husband decided to get a divorce because she found out he was cheating on her. It was a messy deal, and one night Astrid and I came home to her crying after she had just finished smashing her wedding ring in the shop with a hammer.

It was hard to watch her be in so much pain, especially the more I got to know and love her, but amid her pain, we created so many special memories. We had Greek feasts just because, went for walks on the beach to watch the sun come up, drank wine, and danced late at night like goofballs.

I had found my family in a foreign place. After facing loneliness, insecurity, and defeat during my first two years of college, it was in their home where I found freedom from not only my hurt but many of my disordered eating behaviors.

Astrid and June enjoyed eating healthy, yet they also enjoyed some chocolate or ice cream after dinner. One of my favorite brekkies to this day is avocado toast with Vegemite, poached eggs, and kimchi. Making it with Astrid almost every day, I came to believe eating bread first thing in the morning was okay, something I feared before.

She and I also started making smoothie bowls, coming up with all different colors and fruit combinations. She taught me eating healthy can be fun and doesn't always have to involve rules. I think that's why whenever we ate together, I didn't feel stressed and instead felt relieved.

Suddenly, intuitive eating wasn't so difficult. The process was enjoyable and never forced. When it came time to sit down and eat, I was able to focus more on the people and memories being created than I did the food.

This comes back to the point I made earlier: you cannot recover alone.

Almost every night, we'd all cook dinner and help out with setting the table. The first time we did this I offered to pray a blessing, and ever since that day, it was an expected part of dinner time. I'd get three pairs of eyes on me and smiles and head nods encouraging me to pray.

Relaxing and properly digesting my food without a stress response immediately following a meal was so much easier when I lived with Astrid and her family. I rarely had gut flare-ups (a regular part of life before going to Australia) and I felt more at ease than I ever had.

It didn't matter if everyone went to their room after dinner and did their own thing for the rest of the evening. It was the slow process of eating, conversing, and cleaning up after our meal that let me know the day had come to an end and it was okay to rest.

It was the company that let me know I didn't have to work like a dog until midnight, only to give myself five minutes to relax before bed.

I started to find less logic in my habitual practice to stay active and instead accepted my body's response to go to bed early or decompress from the day through writing or coloring.

You see, so much of my eating disorder behaviors came from comparison. I was trying to live up to unrealistic expectations I thought others were living up to, too. Only when I stopped isolating myself and imagining false ways of how others were living did I find freedom from my monsters. This is one area where comparison helped me more than it caged me.

Spontaneity and Small Moments

Astrid taught me how to be spontaneous. Sometimes she would grab an ice cream cone from the freezer in the middle of the afternoon and I'd think, *You can do that?*

We could easily go for a long hike with water, just as easily as we could stop by the bottle shop and pick up mini-champagne bottles to take with us to the top of a hill that overlooked the ocean. Once, we loaded up the car and decided to go camping for two nights out in the bush of northern Australia just because.

Back home, I wouldn't have been able to leave for a trip without completing hard and long workouts leading up to the departure. I'd need to make sure I ate extra "clean" while ensuring I had everything I needed to cater to my eating disorder behaviors while away.

Yet, even though Astrid's brother had workout equipment and a weight bench in the garage I'd occasionally use, it wasn't a big trigger I let control my life or interfere with my relationships because I knew my time there was precious.

Astrid didn't work out in the traditional sense, but we'd swim laps together frequently in an outdoor pool near our home, which worked out great because my knees still weren't back to normal and I had, for the most part, stopped running.

I once had a friend tell me, "If you use nature as your gym, you won't need to go to the gym." This makes me think of Astrid because that's exactly what she exemplified for me.

Not only did she exemplify healthy patterns of living, but she also showed me healthy ways of loving, too. I saw this in the way she cared for her mother, and most of all, in the way she cared for me.

Being transparent with her was easy because she was always transparent with me, and even when we disagreed or thought differently about something, we would still welcome each other's perspective and challenge our own.

The first time I opened up about my eating disorder in-depth was with one of her friends at a community event. This friend spoke so openly about her battle with bulimia, and it gave me a safe place to open up about my struggles as well.

The more I was around her, however, the more I noticed she might still be partaking in old behaviors. One day, I expressed my concern to Astrid, which led to me telling her a good chunk of my story. I surprised myself by doing this and learned vulnerability gets easier the more you practice it.

Astrid and others like her have contributed immensely to my recovery by loving me unconditionally and courageously asking the hard questions I wasn't ready to ask myself.

It's normal to think the help we extend to others isn't much help at all. It's also normal to think helping someone with an addiction, such as an eating disorder, is near impossible. I've been there too but am overcome by those who helped pull me out of disordered eating, even if they didn't know they were helping me, and even if *I* didn't know they were helping me.

When I think back, it wasn't ever grand gestures or big moments leading me to a healthier life. Rather, it was small moments, few words (sometimes none at all), acceptance, and love extended or exemplified by friends, family, and even strangers. That's what brought light to my darkness and helped grow me most.

It is with this realization I'd encourage you to stay hopeful for those you know who are battling an eating disorder or something alike. And if you are the one fighting, I encourage you to not be defeated by an absence of standout moments and huge change.

Remember, it is through the twists and turns, mountains and valleys, that we experience incremental change and long-term growth.

Choosing Recovery Again and Again

Leaving Australia was one of the hardest things I've ever had to do. I had just experienced a whole new world, a world I was in love with and people I was in love with.

After my semester ended, I traveled along the East Coast by myself visiting Brisbane, Surfers Paradise, Byron Bay, and Melbourne. In each place, I met wonderful people, some of which opened up their homes to me.

Before my time abroad, I was so worried I'd lack community. I was worried all the growth I'd made before leaving Oregon would dwindle with time. To my surprise, I came to find the exact opposite. God was so patient with me through my worries, and there were several occasions He gave me awe-inspiring words and images to let me know I wasn't fighting my battles alone.

Even before I left, I was given the assurance my worries were heard. I'll never forget the last church service I was able to make before my trip. I asked I be prayed over for a safe flight, a church community once I got there, unwavering faith as I stayed there, and rest from everything I was working myself up over.

While receiving prayer, I started to get this image of a massive waterfall. I was standing beneath it and getting completely drenched while laughing and smiling. I dismissed the image and thought it was a cliche thing to think of and was most likely just my imagination.

Shortly after, the woman praying for me paused and told me she had received an image of a young girl standing under a big, breathtaking waterfall, joyful and free of worry.

I didn't even know how to respond because of how in sync our encounters were. After telling her I had been given the same image, we hugged and I cried big, ugly tears.

The reason I tell this story is because the waterfall is the image I went back to over and over when I found myself feeling lost and worried while in Australia.

When I doubted my decision of going abroad.
When I struggled to make friends.
When I got the flu.
When I had a week to find somewhere to live.
When I lost my job.
When I had no money to my name.
When I'd wake up with anxiety.
When I couldn't hear anything else but negativity.

Each time, I'd come back to the big, beautiful waterfall and remember myself standing under it and laughing while God told me He wouldn't ever leave or forsake me. He would remind me of the many blessings He still had in store and the multitude of gifts he planned to shower over me, if only I would stop fearing and trust Him.

Throughout my trip, my relationship with Jesus grew tremendously as I watched the waterfall crash over and coat my surroundings in ways so pure I could not deny them.

When I was in Brisbane, I went to a church service and met a man who asked where I was off to next. When I told him I was going to Byron Bay, he gave me the contact info of his friends.

Talk about the coolest, Jesus-loving, hippie couple I've ever met. They picked me up in their van, and I stayed with them for a few days in an old record studio they were living in.

Six months prior, toward the end of my flight to Cairns, a family gave me their contact information and said if I ever came to Melbourne to get in touch with them. Little did I know, they were going to let me stay with them for a whole week absolutely free.

A few months before this, I flew to Sydney for an All Blacks game (a national New Zealand rugby team) and was shown the entire city by the nephew of an older man I met in Baker City, Oregon before my travels. He saw me reading a book on Australia and put me in contact with his nephew in case I ever made it over to Sydney.

Around the same time, I spent a week in Bali with other international students. Soon after that, my friend Kyle came to visit me in Australia, and we snorkeled through the

Great Barrier Reef, drove up to Port Douglas, and explored the rainforest.

I had seen the most incredible views, islands, ocean, and vineyards. And the closer it got to my departure, the more I clung to all of these places, experiences, and people.

The only worry I had by the end of my trip was returning home.

What if I revert to unhealthy patterns?

When I eventually did return home, it was almost like I was pretending to still be living in Australia. Using the same slang terms, cooking the same breakfast I had every day when I was there, and only using stories of my travels as conversation starters.

I felt joyful, yet sad.

In weak moments, my monsters started to tell me it was time to face reality and go back to the life I was living before, but I refused.

No, I've committed to recovery.

Then I asked God one day, "What would it look like for me to have a healthy relationship with food and my body?"

He told me to have a healthy relationship with food and my body would mean to be in full communion with Him, meaning I might not always come in first place with the world.

Letting go of excessive exercise and control of food didn't come immediately, and I still have to be mindful of where the two things land on my priority list. Still, loosening my white-knuckle grip is what began to reveal the peace I had been searching for all along.

It was not about running away; rather, it was about running to the one eager to carry the burdens I held. I believe it's Him who led me to Astrid, June, and the several other people who made me see recovery as possible.

I want to leave you with an encounter I had with God one afternoon during my travels. The experience I had while walking on the beach changed the entire trajectory of my recovery, and afterward, I made a promise that no matter how difficult I found it to move on from my disorder, I wouldn't ever give up.

This memory is what kept me strong each time my monsters chimed in after returning to the US.

No Date
Walking with my toes in the sand, I pray to God and ask Him to please take my hand. Some days this life is easy—filled with smiles, laughs, forgiveness. Other days, things feel heavy—bitter, confusing, anxiety-ridden. So, I sit down and pray. I crouch my head into my legs, letting out tears and hoping my monsters allow a couple of moments for me to hear God clearly. He shows me a patch of yummy strawberries ready to be gobbled up. Then, He shows me the most appealing one in the patch—big, red, and juicy. Why is God showing me strawberries, I wonder? I asked for guidance on what to focus on this season and He's showing me strawberries?

Before I know it, the juicy strawberry is bitten into, the inside revealed; black, moldy, no good. Pretty on the outside and wretched on the inside. I know right away what it means. The strawberry represents me and what God wants to say becomes known: outward appearances are tempting and alluring, yet it's heart posture and inward appearance He's most concerned with. During this season I'm meant to stop searching for security in exercise, food, and the way I present myself to the world. Instead, I'm meant to focus on my heart and finding contentment in Jesus. That's where I'll find the rest, fulfillment, and strength I've been praying for.

Recovery is not a one-time thing. Similar to forgiveness, it's something we must do again and again. And recovering doesn't mean you never have a bad body image again, or you never get enticed by the idea of turning to an old behavior for comfort. Those things *will* happen, and they will happen regularly.

But recovery is an act of resistance. It's understanding the lies you lived by for so long, and when they come up, acknowledging their presence and choosing to cope in new ways. It's speaking (not suppressing) your feelings so before they manifest into truths you believe, they're broken and you can see them with fresh eyes. It's saying, *This is hard, but I'm going to keep fighting.*

It's losing a false identity and source of control, and it's gaining a life.

CHAPTER 16

SURRENDERING CONTROL

———

I want to be more grounded in my identity and okay with the idea of not everyone liking me. I want to like myself.

I used to, and sometimes still do, live under the lie that my worth is dependent on how much I do or don't do.

Did I read my Bible?
Did I pray for all those people who I promised I would?
Did I meal prep this week?
Have I posted on Instagram lately?
Am I being too judgmental?
How am I working to grow my faith?
Is my wardrobe up to date? What would make it better?
Is my workout routine hard enough? How can I make it more challenging?

I stress and fret over the tension of living in our modern world and following a life worthy of the One who set me free, glazing over the most important thing: I have been set free.

You have been set free.

That is only a small list of things that run through my head daily... and that is only one list.

I have lists dedicated toward all kinds of things—chores I have to do, friends I should reach out to, things I want to buy, places I want to eat, names for my future kids, movies I'd like to watch, books I'd like to read, books I've already read, groceries I'm out of, and reminders telling me to paint my toes, relax, and settle down.

The biggest problem with my lists is that oftentimes painting my toes, relaxing, and settling down often get pushed to the side. The other problem is my lists are filled with dozens of wants or needs. Lately, I've been trying to make more meaningful lists that, instead of encouraging me to do, do, do, remind me to slow down, take a breath, and rest. Being content with all of which I've already done and have.

It's hard.

My Type A personality is what fueled my eating disorder behaviors and made recovery seem impossible at times.

Stepping on the scale each morning and evening and seeing a number lower than the day before made me feel powerful.

It meant I was following all the rules set before me by society, strangers, and my monsters.

Give a Type A personality an A, and nothing will stop them.

There have been so many moments in my life where my superficial acts—my pretending and distraction—were all I knew. I'm really good at being busy and even better at making people think I have it all together by proving to them how much I can accomplish and do.

Look at me. I'm balanced. My life is organized. I have it all together.

This isn't and never was true. I don't have it all together. I have some of it together, sure. Other times, I need a big kick in the butt to push me out of my striving because perfection is impossible, and it's chasing after perfection that yanks me out of resting and being. It leaves me empty and deprived of all life's pleasure.

My eating disorder never let me sleep in. It would wake me when my eyes were still tired, and it would drag me out of the house while my feet slowly pedaled behind and tried to keep up with the harsh demands to run faster.

My monsters would flash red lights over every dessert table, and alongside every social encounter was a label that read "PROVE YOURSELF."

In recovery, I meet perfection in the precious moments when life slows down, when I'm not reaching for a goal, stretched thin by commitments, and seeking improvement. I greet it and say "Hello," but the choice to follow after it is ultimately my choice. Most days, I choose not to.

Now if you are a doer like me, please don't go thinking there is something wrong with you and you need to change. That's not at all what I'm saying. The problem isn't being a doer; the problem is aiming to be perfect. Brené Brown calls perfection a defense move, and I agree with her.

> Perfectionism is a defense move. It's the belief that if we do things perfectly and look perfect, we can minimize or avoid the pain of blame, judgment, and shame. Perfectionism is a twenty-ton shield we lug around thinking it will protect us, when in fact it's the thing that's really preventing us from being seen.[53]

I think there is something unique and special about the doers of our world and the determination they bring into the paths they take, and I believe God designed doers for a reason. He makes no mistakes, especially when it comes to how we were created. Just like any other personality type, however, who we are often gets warped by our world and over time, this takes a toll on our motives.

You see, my to-do lists often have an invisible tag on them that reads *"earn acceptance,"* and I have a habit of forgetting approval has already been crossed off my list. Our status in

---

53 Brené Brown, *Daring Greatly: How the Courage to Be Vulnerable Transforms the Way We Live, Love, Parent, and Lead* (New York: Avery Publishing, 2012), 129.

God's eyes does not waver. It does not expire. It is a holy and eternal promise.

Searching for My Role

I went into high school with this idea I had to do everything. I wanted to be recognized not only for my looks, but my talent as well, and I wanted to be good at something but didn't know what that something was. At first, I thought it could be volleyball.

After my eighth-grade year had ended, I spent the summer before high school practicing my volleyball skills and was determined to make my freshman year worthwhile. After hours upon hours practicing, I ended up making the junior varsity team.

I fell in love with volleyball so much freshman year, I decided I didn't even want to play basketball anymore. However, when you are 5'11" in a small town, you don't have much of a choice as to whether you play basketball. Especially not me, someone who was known by the coaches and friends with a lot of the girls who played.

But at the time, I couldn't stop thinking about how volleyball could be my golden ticket out of the town I grew up in.

My parents never started a savings account for me, and they never discussed my continued education when I was younger. Both my mom and my dad dropped out in high school, and I think their only wish was I would graduate.

So, my plan was to graduate high school and do something big with my life. Most adults around made it seem like that "big" thing was college, and because I wanted to adhere to expectations, I started dedicating most of my free time to athletics—specifically volleyball—in hopes I could get a scholarship.

Little did I know, God had other plans ahead. Still, I relentlessly pressed into my own and was left unsatisfied every time.

The comparison plague I mentioned earlier only got more pronounced when I entered high school, and it hit me incredibly hard during sports. I compared myself to how good my teammates were, the way they looked versus how I looked, how the coaches responded to them versus how they responded to me, their boyfriends, their friends, their belongings, and their natural abilities.

Everywhere I looked, I saw room for improvement, and somewhere along the way, I began believing the narrative that to be "good" meant to be perfect. I had to have everything I saw in everyone around me. I needed to be more disciplined and work harder.

My monsters would be on the bleachers at my games yelling, *You suck!* every time I made a mistake or got pulled off the court and replaced with someone else.

This led me to seek out other clubs and extracurriculars so I was always busy. Always headed to a meeting. Always working on a project. Always trying to find my thing.

That's why I clung so tightly to my eating disorder. I excelled at it.

The number one tool to help me recover from my perfectionistic mindset and eating disorder, however, has been the Enneagram. It's given me guidance on how to grow out of my Oneness and toward more wholeness, which is why you will see me quote the words of Ian Morgan Cron and Suzanne Stabile, two Enneagram experts, throughout this chapter.

They explain in such concrete detail the manic episodes I've experienced trying to meet perfection. In *The Road Back to You* they write:

> From the time they get up to the time they lie down, Ones perceive a world rife with errors and feel a bounden duty to correct it...They chase perfection because they have this vague, unsettling feeling if they make a mistake, someone is going to jump out to blame, criticize, or punish them.[54]

Looking back, I see how in high school, I tried to achieve too much at once, which only left me feeling tired, drained, and burnt out. No matter how hard I tried to be successful at everything, I failed.

I have a tendency, when I set my mind on something, to not focus on anything else. It is hard for me to multi-task and be committed—or rather perfect—at more than one thing. This is where I felt the most tension in high school and eventually

---

54 Cron and Stabile, *The Road Back to You*, 93.

college. I was striving to be everyone I wasn't because I didn't know who I was.

Sometimes, I still find myself trying to tackle all I can. I go through unhealthy seasons where envy runs wild and I ache to experience the same sort of contentment I see others experiencing.

When freshman year ended and sophomore year arrived, I was especially caught in the *do more, be better* cycle.

Three months of summer had given me plenty of time to gain momentum and chase various goals and things I had planned for my sophomore year of high school.

I spent the summer working on my volleyball skills again, but unlike my freshman year of high school, volleyball wasn't as enjoyable for me anymore. Many of the things I once let go unnoticed started to bother me more than ever. The politics and favoritism, the gossip, the drama, the cheering, screaming, and smiling we had to do even when we were losing significantly.

When it came time for the season to end, I was eager and looked forward to basketball season. I made varsity and thought for sure this was God telling me, *You need to go and get a scholarship in basketball! This is what I made you for.*

And maybe basketball could have been the path I took, but it's not the one I chose. My sophomore year on the court brought tears, frustration, little success, and low self-esteem.

I didn't get a lot of playing time. I bounced between the JV and varsity team because I rode the line of being good but not good enough, and it seemed I didn't even have a team at times. What I had was potential, the willingness to try, to never give up, and a constant motivator by the name of envy.

I'd get to my car after a game and break down bawling. Sometimes I'd let out tears before making it to my car. Teammates or coaches would notice I was upset, and when they tried to talk to me about it, it was like an entire dam had broken loose.

The thing is, I was never mad at my coaches or my teammates. Instead, I was mad at myself and because I'd internalize so many of my emotions, keeping them in was not easy.

> All of us have a reproachful voice that gets triggered from time to time when we do something stupid and then it goes away. As a rule, Ones have a merciless inner critic; unlike ours, it never goes away. It's punishing. It's relentless.[55]

I wanted to contribute to the success of my team, to be trusted on the court, cheered on and celebrated. I wanted to feel confident in my role and never did.

My whole life, I've felt that I have to try much harder than those around me. With school, sports, relationships, looks. When experiences like the ones I had in basketball came, I felt defeated.

---

55 Cron and Stabile, The Road Back to You, 96.

Being older, I know I felt this way because of the high demand I put on myself to be perfect. I was so busy looking at others, I never took time to look at myself and notice my own accomplishments and gifts.

If you've dealt with your own monsters, you know criticism on top of their voices cuts deep. Cron and Stabile put it this way:

> Given the stream of negative self-commentary their inner critic levels at them all day, Ones don't receive criticism well... Though very sensitive to criticism themselves, Ones are shocked when you tell them you feel like they're being harshly critical of you. Seriously? You're only being given a thimble-sized sample of the bitter self-recrimination they drink from every day.[56]

When I finally did start to find my place on the court, there was a new girl in the grade below me, Mae, who came to one of our open gyms. She was tall like me, absolutely stunning, and extremely kind. She was also faster than almost every girl on the varsity team, skinny, and strong.

The year I got placed on varsity and also swung down to JV, she too was assigned the same role. Mae and I ended up really good friends and hung out often outside of basketball. But on the court, I despised her talent.

I saw how the coaches reacted when she outran and outrebounded all the girls who had played basketball their whole

---

56   Cron and Stabile, The Road Back to You, 99.

lives. I saw how my teammates cheered her on. Since we played the same position, I also got to see her each time the coaches put her in over me, and each time I messed up and she came in to fill my position. Some games, I was lucky to even get a minute.

What upset me most was that I knew all the plays we ran like the back of my hand and studied them in my free time to make sure I was prepared for games. I went to one-on-one coaching sessions, stayed late after practice to work on my free throws, and tried my absolute hardest to be ready for every practice and game.

Mae didn't know any of the plays. She would get lost out on the court and look side to side like a deer in the headlights. I never saw her doing any of the things I did to excel, and it bothered me to my core because *here I am working so hard only to be replaced by someone with all of the natural abilities I wasn't given.*

Again, I loved Mae and I was closest to her out of everyone on my team. I didn't resent her; I resented the fact I *wasn't* her. She was so wholesome and had the biggest heart that when she sensed I was upset (because I'm the worst at hiding my feelings), she would apologize.

"I don't know why they keep putting me in when I don't even know what I'm doing," she would say. "You were doing so good... he shouldn't have pulled you out."

She was humble, similar to Rosie, and wouldn't ever admit her talent. This made me want to avoid the comparison plague, yet even when I tried, my coaches would unknowingly compare me to her.

These moments caused me to ruminate on every small detail of who I was.

Maybe if I looked like Mae and was more athletic, I'd get more playing time.
Maybe if I was more outgoing or funny.
Maybe if I was less serious. Less emotional. Less me.

Looking back, I wish I had remembered Amy Morin's important words during those moments. She writes:

> It's easy to think someone has a great life from the outside, but you never know what sort of battle they're fighting on the inside. It's not fair to compare the way your life really is to the way you perceive someone else's life to be.[57]

As I've started opening up to others about my eating disorder, I've had so many people tell me, "I had no idea" or, "I just thought you were really into fitness and liked to eat healthy."

We are good at wearing masks, putting on the version of us we think other people want to see when really, we are dying on the inside. Perhaps that's why it takes so long for people to come to the conclusion that they are battling something as serious as a mental illness. We become so good at hiding that we trick even ourselves.

---

57   Morin, *13 Things Mentally Strong Women Don't Do*, 18.

And although Mae didn't have a mental illness (that I know of), she had her own battles. We all do.

Striving for Perfection

I often feel the same as I did playing basketball when I see those around me crushing goals, excelling in their careers, and having all the answers (so it seems), while I can't even decide what to eat when I go out to lunch with a friend. I feel so much weight on my shoulders to strive toward everything because I don't know my thing. To be everyone because I feel like no one.

It seems I always try harder and work longer because I fear that if I don't, I will be left behind. It's a responsibility I took on at a young age when such a lie was true, and I *did* have to try harder and work longer than most kids my age. Not only that, but I've started to recognize that this narrative is part of how I'm wired.

> Growing up, Ones try to be model kids. They know the rules and follow them to the letter. They spend lots of energy comparing themselves to other kids... This comparing and judging mind remains with Ones their entire lives... The wounding message little Ones pick up is that they have to "be good" or do things "right." Mistakes are unacceptable. People and things are either perfect or wrong. Period.[58]

I have a difficult time deciphering what I want at a restaurant, in a job, in a man, and other everyday decisions because I'm

---

58   Cron and Stabile, The Road Back to You, 101-102.

so easily enticed by the wants and roles of others. Indecision has this crippling effect that leaves me feeling unsure of who I am and unsatisfied with what is already in front of me.

Whether it be my reflection, my grades, people, possessions, food, love—I always seem to scope out room for improvement.

I could be better
It could be better
They could be better
This could all be better.

In each situation thinking, *Surely, after I perfect this one thing, all will be well.*

In recent years, God keeps bringing to mind the refreshing truth that I don't have control over as much as I'd like to think I do.

I'm pretty sure He's been shaking his head as He watches me write my to-do lists, explain myself to others, and take extensive notes on just about every book I read as if I might be quizzed later. Giggling at my made-up ideas of what could be and asking me to slow down and focus on what already is.

> No matter how you look at it, One's crusade to perfect the world is a fool's errand. There's always an unmade bed in it somewhere. Until they begin a spiritual journey, they'll never know a minute's peace.[59]

---

59   Cron and Stabile, The Road Back to You, 98.

I'm reminded that if I'm always waiting for things to be right and the world to be perfect, I won't ever be happy. I don't have to be everyone because I am someone. I'm a daughter—a queen—crowned by the King most high.

You are enough, He whispers.

There's no striving to be done, the work is finished.

My name is Carly, and His name is Hope.

Altered Expectations

I don't think God is mad I have an eye for improvement. I just think He might be sad when I fail to recognize the perfection He brings into each situation I face; the peaceful presence that is error-free, all around me, and never failing.

In every sport I played when I was younger, I was recognized as Most Improved. At the time, I didn't feel like the award was all that special and quite honestly, it made me feel embarrassed.

Now everyone knows I used to be much worse than I am now. Now everyone is probably comparing my first game to my last one thinking, "Did she even improve?"
Now everyone is going to have high expectations for me to keep improving, and what if this is as good as it gets?

Being the MVP (most valuable player) or best offensive or defensive player sounded so much better because the people awarded those had a real role. I didn't feel I had a role as the most improved player other than the same role as the entire team. *Haven't we all improved from the beginning to the end of the season?* I wondered.

Getting recognized as most improved felt like a slap in the face because after working so hard to be recognized as someone, I was recognized as everyone. It felt like missing the bus by seconds, failing to reach your destination in time, and then having to run to the next stop as quickly as you can and still having the door shut on you. It felt like exhaustion and frustration and anger and shame.

I understand now the slap I felt from the most improved awards given to me when I was younger were caused by a false belief that I had to get it right and establish my role on the team. Instead of seeing improvement as a gift and blessing to be thankful for, I saw it as a never-ending quest that was mine to conquer and wouldn't ever be achieved.

Improvement is certainly a gift and something to be thankful for. Chasing perfection, on the other hand, is unrealistic and only a demand forced on me by myself and by my monsters. Improvement can happen without us noticing it—when we are just living our lives—but trying to attain perfection causes us to obsess over the tiniest details that aren't worth our energy.

When I was younger, I held an idea that didn't match reality. I thought only when I was perfect at my role (whatever that role was) should I be recognized as anyone. That's the issue with comparison. You end up comparing yourself to so many people you never reach the finish line.

Picking out from each person the "thing" they have and the "thing" you want causes you to forget no one has all of the "things."

Sometimes, to improve might mean to fail. Trying out different roles to discover your role and believing that even when you do fall or take a couple hits, there will still be people in the crowd cheering you on. It takes believing grace requires nothing of you, and you don't have to know all the answers.

We are always improving and, if we follow Jesus, always working to be more like Him in everything we do. Yet, it's challenging to stop running toward the finish line of perfection even when you do believe in Jesus because a lot of our world is still running.

It's hard to wrap your head around the truth Jesus is perfect and, by His sacrifice, is making us perfect, too.

In the book of James, it reads, "And then as your endurance grows even stronger it will release perfection into every part of your being until there is nothing missing and nothing lacking."[60]

The finish line of perfection has already been crossed in the kingdom of God, and the more we cling to Him through the trials life presents us, the less we view life as a race we have to win. We have endurance, are patient, and begin to realize with God we are perfect in the sense that we are complete. We are not wanting or needing anything because we are mature in our faith. That's the kind of perfection I want.

---

60 James 1:4 (The Passion Translation).

Still, checkpoints of improvement are to be celebrated because with each one, we are aiming closer to the life God destined for us from the beginning.

The more I understand who He made me to be, the more capable I am of accepting and admiring who God made those around me to be as well. I can be both confident in who I am and who I am not, which are equally as important.

Our identity is not rooted in the shifting sands of the labels other people give us. Our identity is rooted in Christ and the sturdy foundation He's built for us.

Remember, there is a broad path many will take in this life, and a narrow path only a few will choose.[61] In my story, the broad path is the mentality that I have to be in control, perfect, and put together.

The narrow path, on the other hand, is going against this mentality while resting in the truth that I'm good enough. I know this is the narrow path because it doesn't always come naturally. It's an intentional choice and a specific way of living.

In Romans 12, Paul outlines beautifully how we are to take the narrow path:

> Therefore, I urge you, brothers and sisters, in view of God's mercy, to offer your bodies as a living sacrifice, holy and pleasing to God—this is your true and proper worship. Do not conform to the pattern of this world

---

61 Matt. 7:13-14 (ESV).

but be transformed by the renewing of your mind. Then you will be able to test and approve what God's will is—his good, pleasing and perfect will.[62]

Paul goes on to compare the human body to our role in the body of Christ. God designed the body in a way where each organ has its own role and function so it may work accordingly. Similarly, we all have our own role and function in this world designed by Him.

And it is silly to believe we have the responsibility of fulfilling *every* role. That is not His expectation for us. We each have gifts we are meant to use and use well, but we weren't ever meant to do it all.

> We have different gifts, according to the grace given to each of us. If your gift is prophesying, then prophesy in accordance with your faith; if it is serving, then serve; if it is teaching, then teach; if it is to encourage, then give encouragement; if it is giving, then give generously; if it is to lead, do it diligently; if it is to show mercy, do it cheerfully.[63]

How I interpret this part of Romans and what it goes on to say in chapter twelve is only when we are fulfilling our role in the kingdom and not trying to fulfill all of the roles are we able to let our love be genuine while honoring one another.

---

62 Rom. 12:1-2 (New International Version).
63 Rom. 12:6-8 (NIV).

I don't think there is any harm in wanting to learn or master gifts outside our knowledge, yet we don't have to be taken down or dread our responsibility to keep up with the heaviness of striving after all things, like how I felt when I got awarded for being most improved.

I think what Paul is saying is our passion will be intensified when we start to know our role and purpose, hold fast to He who is good, and readily embrace the spirit of God who lives in us. We are most passionate when we are joyful in hope, patient in affliction, and faithful in prayer.[64]

When I begin to think with sober judgment, I do not see or expect perfection from myself because I start to see myself according to the measure of faith God has assigned. My expectations for myself and others start to match the Father's, and my yardstick of judgment shortens.

The responsibility of perfection and judgment is not on me, on myself, or others. My job is to align with the will of God, which is good, acceptable, and perfect. To resemble Jesus' perfection to the best of my ability, but to also accept the lifelong process is to follow Him. We won't always get it right, and we aren't expected to.

Embracing Who You Already Are

Did you know in the book of Ephesians there are twenty-four identity statements within only the first three chapters of the book, telling you who you already are and what you've

---

64 Rom. 12:9-12 (NIV).

already been given in Christ? Without works, by just living and breathing, you are in Christ:

1. Blessed
2. Chosen
3. Holy
4. Blameless
5. Predestined
6. Adopted
7. Redeemed
8. Forgiven
9. Given an Inheritance
10. Sealed with the promised Holy Spirit
11. Loved
12. Alive
13. Saved
14. Raised up
15. Seated with God in the heavenly places
16. Workmanship created in Jesus for good works
17. Brought near by the blood of Christ
18. Made one with Christ
19. Reconciled
20. Given access in one Spirit
21. A fellow citizen with the saints
22. A member of the household of God
23. Built together into a dwelling place for God by the Spirit
24. Given boldness and access with confidence[65]

---

65 Eph. 1:3-3:12 (ESV).

These are things that, if you've accepted Jesus into your heart as Lord and Savior, you cannot change. No matter what you do, you have these things in Christ.

I've been reading this list of words over myself ever since committing to recovery and still have yet to fully absorb them. Why? Because it takes time to believe there is a God who loves me so much that—even by knowing all of the places I've been wrong and ran astray—He still loves me, has chosen me, finds me blameless, and on down the list.

The same is true of you. You're blessed, holy, and sealed with the promised Holy Spirit.

Satan loves to tell us to obtain these gifts we have to work for them. All through my eating disorder, he told me I had to prove myself through perfection and performance, and I believed him, but that's not true, and that's not from God.

Jesus already paid the price for you and me. Recognizing this has transformed my life, and as I continue to practice believing it, I'm confident the voices in my head will quiet themselves and God will reveal Himself in a new way.

When who you are starts to get lost in the noise of the world (and your monsters), read these twenty-four identity statements over yourself. Similar to the "I am" affirmations, you can write these on sticky notes and pin them by your mirror, or in a place you find yourself often.

Also remember this: freedom is not found in what you do, but in who you are.

CHAPTER 17

RECOVERY IN REST

———

When my mind goes from one place to the next, it often keeps me from God's presence. It's when I slow down I become less anxious, when I really sit and allow His love in to take care of me. This doesn't mean my problems disappear, yet they do become secondary to my security in Him.

Recovery is not an overnight fix. It is hard and it hurts. Sometimes it feels like taking twenty steps forward. Other days, it feels like taking a hundred steps backward. I've been told it takes, on average, three to ten years to fully heal from an eating disorder. Me? I'm only in my fourth year.

I feel I'm most aware of my progress in recovery when I'm most unaware of my striving. Like the day I'm writing this, for instance. For lunch, I ate a buffalo chicken dish with carrots and fingerling potatoes. Then, for an afternoon snack, I ate carrots again with hummus.

Two servings of carrots within four hours? That would have most certainly broken one of my food rules when my eating disorder was in full swing because *why would I have two servings of carrots when I only have so much volume I'm allowed to consume every day? Plus, repeating the same color of food is not okay... and carrots have sugar in them.*

But I didn't even notice I consumed two servings of carrots until right before sitting down to write this at 10:00 p.m. That's growth.

I break food rules all the time now, sometimes with guilt, and other times with freedom. It's part of following my intuition, exploring both the positive and negative feelings of recovery, and healing somewhere along the way.

Through it all, there is Jesus. Waiting patiently, waiting for you. Whatever mess you're in, whatever trial you are facing, He is there and ready to listen whenever you are ready to let Him in.

A good way to start letting Him into your heart is to simply have a conversation, similar to a conversation you might have with a friend. Pull up a chair and imagine Jesus right there sitting across from you. Tell Him about your day... your frustrations. Tell Him what you're grateful for... what you're hoping for.

Tell Him you're sorry for all of the times you thought you knew best and came to find out you didn't know anything, for the times you got caught striving to achieve an identity apart from the one you've already been given in Him. Then, listen. What does Jesus want to say to you? What does He want you to know?

Quiet your mind, put away your phone, and just be still for a moment. It may not happen the first time, but if you keep showing up, He will too.

My Line in the Sand Moment

There was a line in the sand moment when God pointed out I was missing a major key ingredient in my recovery: forgiveness. Not forgiveness toward others, but forgiveness toward myself.

I had spent the year before working to reclaim my relationship with my body, exercise, and food.

I threw away my scale and stopped weighing myself.
I got rid of my "too small" clothes I knew I couldn't ever wear again if I was to be healthy, and I got new ones to fit my body.
I started taking yoga classes and fell in love with the inward and outward strength I felt from it.
I refused to do any assignment in my college courses that required me to track my food and calorie intake.
I met up with other eating disorder survivors regularly to swap stories and learn from each other over a meal.
I did things that scared me, like pastoring a community of people in my church weekly.
I read self-help books, listened to podcasts, and practiced vulnerability daily.
I even chopped off all of my hair to embrace the new me.

But I avoided the hardest part of recovery (for me), which was coming face-to-face with my brokenness and saying, "I love you."

Hearing something you've failed to do is harsh, and hearing something you don't want to do is even harsher. I was nervous to ask God how I was supposed to forgive myself. It seemed there were tips and to-do's for just about everything else in my recovery journey, and now I felt stuck. Still, I pressed on. *I can't go back now.*

Around the same time, I felt called to singleness. Specifically, I felt called to be joyful in my singleness, to see it as a gift rather than a burden. To do this, I first needed to heal, and to heal I needed to go back to what was going through my head during my eating disorder. Not to relive the past, but to understand the girl who was hungry for more, the girl who felt shattered into a million pieces and unable to put herself back together.

I've saved all of my journals from the time I was eight years old and now have a big tote full of them. One night, I drug this tote out and set a stack of journals on the floor. On my seventeenth birthday, Rosie gifted me one hand-decorated journal for every month of the year—twelve total.

I decided these twelve journals would be a good place to start understanding myself, since I was given them at the start of the more intense days of my eating disorder, right after I moved out of Rosie's and in with my grandparents.

I'd always kept a journal but could only recall a few times I revisited specific entries.

It became my evening ritual to make my way through the journals by reading a handful of entries before bed. For every entry that mentioned body, food, and exercise in a shameful way, I'd place a blue sticky note at the top of the page. This was my attempt to still make progress in my journey while ignoring the initial request from God.

You see, I finally did ask God, *How do I forgive myself?* And when I asked that question, He brought my journals to mind, the way I hid from others in the pages, afraid to let myself be seen. Then He asked me to destroy all of the entries where I mentioned myself not being good enough.

I couldn't do it. I got mad at God.

Why would He ask me to destroy the very things I hold dear?
My journals are important to me.
I want generations below me to one day be given them for comfort and guidance.

Only, when I thought about that statement more deeply, I wasn't so sure. *Do I really want my grandkids, or later their kids, to have to read about the remorse I had for my own body and being?*

The answer was simple: no. At least, not in that depth. My story is important, and I do want generations below me to know not all of life is happy, feel-good experiences, but they will see that through plenty of my other entries.

So, why was it so difficult for me to destroy the entries?

For one: I didn't know how to do that without ruining the other pages of the journal.

For two: I was terrified to let them go.

For three: I was attached to the entries because I now had compassion for the younger me who felt she wasn't good enough.

This is what led to me marking pages with blue sticky notes. Before I got rid of them completely, I needed closure. I needed to go back to that place just once more.

I'd shed tears as I reread entries, understanding the power of words in a whole new way.

I lived by myself at this time, so I kept the journals stacked in my bedroom in case I tried to escape the evening ritual I committed to. I did the same thing after I was finished reading the entries, only now they were in the living room.

If I had it my way, I would've carefully placed them back in the tote and moved on to more exciting things like a novel or Netflix. But the healing wasn't done. My running and distraction, on the other hand, was.

So, the journal entries sat, and sat, and sat.

Then, one morning I was praying and saw the dusty journals with their blue sticky notes.

I crawled over to where they were on the floor and brought the stack next to my coffee table.

Then I said to Jesus, *I'm going to do this, but I need you here with me because I can't do it alone.*

We sat together on the floor that morning, as he rubbed my back in the most gentle way and whispered in my ear softly, *I will never leave or forsake you.*

I began tearing each highlighted entry out from the binding of the journals, feeling all the feelings to come up, weeping, repenting, and forgiving with each torn page.

And Jesus wept with me. He felt everything I was feeling because He is compassionate and merciful. Reminding me, *I know this is hard now, but this is where freedom begins.*

Burning Down Lies and Embracing Freedom

Ripping out my journal entries was without a doubt one of the most transformative moments in my recovery, and I truly did feel strongholds that had controlled me for so long released and let go of that day. Yet, I knew the journey didn't stop there because when God asked me to get rid of the entries, he didn't just mean rip them out of my journals while still holding on to their lies. Instead, he asked me to destroy them completely.

About five months later, I decided to go on a silence and solitude retreat by myself at our family's beach house in Lincoln City, Oregon.

I arrived on a Friday with my duffel bag, snacks, and all twelve of my journals. My two-day silence and solitude retreat involved detaching from my phone, music, and TV, practicing something called Lectio Devina (a slow and focused way of reading and meditating on scripture), writing this book, reading, and being with God.

The trip also involved destroying my journals. Although the other reasons for being there were meaningful, I knew that was the real reason I showed up.

When I arrived, I built a fire in the woodstove to keep warm, walked over to the grocery store to get a few items, enjoyed a nice dinner, worked on the book you're now holding in your hands, and painted my nails. It wasn't until 11:00 p.m. when I finally mustered up the courage to start a conversation with God.

Down on my knees near the fire, I didn't even know what to say. It had been so long since I first agreed to go on this journey, and I was finally there. I started by thanking Jesus for being so patient with me, for guiding me, for loving me endlessly, for being my friend, and for walking beside me like He promised He would.

I then started to read back through a few of the entries before I tossed them into the fire and said goodbye to them forever. And as I read, I saw the torn pages with a new set of eyes. No longer deceived but set free. I couldn't wait to get rid of them.

I carefully lit the edge of one of the sheets of paper and watched it turn from white to brown to black, devoured by flames and turned into ash. I then lit another, and another, and another, crumpling the pieces of paper now and throwing them into the fire.

I expected to be sad, for an overflow of tears and built-up emotion to pour out onto the floor in front of me like the day I tore out the pages. And I did have some tears, only they were not sad tears.

With each piece of paper I watched disintegrate in the fire, I felt joy and release. Weights lifted. In a way, I felt like I had already done the hard part of trusting Jesus when all I wanted to do was run. Although it had taken me so long to get rid of the journal entries once and for all, it was like He hadn't ever stopped working on my heart. He had prepared me for that moment.

When I burned the journal entries, He clapped and rejoiced at the defeat of the lies I had clung to for so long and let warp my identity.

Before going to bed that night, I sat by the fire and wrote this:

Light and Lifted: Silence and Solitude Retreat Day 1
I feel light. I feel lifted. I feel cared for. You make me light. You lift me up. You care in ways I have yet to understand. A year ago, You asked me to get rid of journal entries I was clinging to that specifically targeted my weight, body goals, how I was going to alter both of those things, hopes I had to be noticed and heard, and my plans to prove myself to others. I wrote in one entry how I felt trapped, and I was trapped. Alone in lies and unable to hear or listen to you clearly.

Last year the thought of getting rid of those entries felt impossible, but tonight I didn't feel that way. I was expecting to be an emotional mess, similar to before when the only thing continuing to help me through the process was Your gentle hand rubbing my back. Tonight, I still feel Your comfort but instead, feel joy. I feel weights being lifted, lies being destroyed, and a new beginning positioning itself beautifully. I realize I was just as ready to get rid of those entries as You were. It took me much longer but as always, Your goodness came to delight my weakness.

Thank you, Father, for building me up, for strengthening me in Your truth, and for reminding me that I do not have to perform, prove, work harder, or get it right 100 percent of the time. Thank you, Father, that the victory is Yours and Yours always. I know I have access to You whenever I choose and the only time I believe differently is when I'm looking through foggy lenses in need of cleaning. You are as close to me as the hairs on my head.

I hope to continue growing in the direction of healing as 2019 approaches, and I ask you to continue to guard me and keep me safe in Your arms when things get tough. Helping me to embrace the good parts of my personality and to accept and learn from the not so fun parts. I'm not sure what the next year has in store but I'm up for all You have in mind. Whether it be a relationship, singleness, more healing, celebration. Where you go, I go. Sometimes unwilling at first... but eventually following so closely I'm stepping on your heels. I love you.

The next day, I woke up to the sun shining and a beautiful blue sky.

After a morning spent drinking good coffee, reading, and praying, I walked down to the beach and found a nice spot up against a tree in the dry sand where I read, drank some more coffee, and curled up in a blanket for a couple of hours.

I found during my time away that it's in the stillness and silence where we find Love eager to wrap us in His arms. God is always speaking to us, and He is always at work. All we have to do to hear Him is slow down and listen.

For me, slowing down and listening meant getting away from my normal element and getting in tune with the Spirit. I didn't know what was going to happen in the silence and solitude, but it was when I stopped trying to perfect and control the things around me I gained the most provision: words to direct how I am to handle the past, the present, and the future.

Rest

Once a week, you'll find me with sleepy eyes, a cup of coffee in one hand, and a book in the other. My phone will be tucked away or on silent, and I'll spend until after lunchtime in my robe trying to awaken my spirit after a week's worth of work. I'll wrap up my reading and make a delicious brunch, usually something I've been craving all week like French toast.

I'll maybe go for a walk or do some yoga, whatever my body is asking for that day. Then I'll take a hot bath and probably sing to some worship music while I wash my hair. Most likely I'll stay in the bath for close to an hour after, reading some more and sipping on a yummy beverage of my choice.

This day is set apart. There are no plans, no to-do's, no food rules, no social media, and no wanting or worrying. The only rules are sleep in, avoid anything that feels like work, acknowledge God in everything you do, and rest. This is Sabbath and it has changed my life.

If you don't know what the Sabbath is, it is one full day where you put into action this commandment:

> Remember the Sabbath day, to keep it holy. Six days you shall labor, and do all your work, but the seventh day is a Sabbath to the Lord your God. On it, you shall not do any work.... For in six days the Lord made heaven and earth, the sea, and all that is in them, and rested on the seventh day. Therefore, the Lord blessed the Sabbath day and made it holy.[66]

In John Mark Comer's words, "The Sabbath is simply a day to stop: stop working, stop wanting, stop worrying, just *stop*."[67]

The old me would have scoffed at this. *Rest? I don't have time. I'm busy. There's too much to be done. Maybe when I'm not in school. Maybe when I don't have so much on my plate.*

Little did I know, the Sabbath is what fuels me to go out and accomplish all the things on my plate. Ever since I've been practicing it, the other days of the week come with

---

66 Exod. 20:8-11 (ESV).

67 John Mark Comer, *The Ruthless Elimination of Hurry: How to Stay Emotionally Healthy and Spiritually Alive in the Chaos of the Modern World* (London: Hodder & Stoughton, 2019), 148.

more ease. And when they feel grueling, I remind myself I only have a short time until I get to hit the pause button for twenty-four hours.

If God was able to rest after creating the entire world, then I certainly can, too. Plus, it's been proven productivity plummets when we overwork ourselves. All hurry does is make us less productive.[68]

Rachel Hollis mentions this in *Girl, Wash Your Face:*

> Our bodies are incredible. They can do unbelievable things. They will also tell you exactly what they need if you're willing to listen. And if you're not, if you try to do too many things without rest, they will absolutely shut down to get what they need.[69]

During my recovery from an eating disorder, I've also been recovering from something called hurry sickness.

It turns out my eating disorder and hurry were close pals, and because of this, it gave the enemy even more of an opportunity to deceive me. In *The Ruthless Elimination of Hurry,* Comer says:

> Today you're far more likely to run into the enemy in a form of an alert on your phone while you're reading your Bible or a multiday Netflix binge or a full-on dopamine addiction to Instagram or a Saturday

---

68 Comer, The Ruthless Elimination of Hurry, 154.
69 Hollis, *Girl, Wash Your Face*, 26.

morning at the office or *another* soccer game on a Sunday or commitment after commitment after commitment in a life of speed.[70]

A life of speed is what made the idea of recovery so unappealing, yet what I realized is I was always hurrying to get to the things that bring me the most joy like writing, reading, a beautiful view, a hike, good food, or a chance to catch up with people I love.

I had to create space for these things or else they never would have happened because there's *always* something else you could be doing.

> Following Jesus has to make it on to your schedule and into your practices or it will simply never happen. Apprenticeship to Jesus will remain an idea, not a reality in your life.[71]

In time, I found the Sabbath was a way to reconnect with myself, to reconnect with God, walk the world slowly, and lean into my intuition.

It has especially helped me recover from exercise addiction. Not instantly but over time I've eliminated any kind of high-intensity movement on the Sabbath.

The rhythm I set for that one day a week allowed me to check in with myself on all other days of the week. *What is my*

---

70 Comer, The Ruthless Elimination of Hurry, 20.
71 Comer, The Ruthless Elimination of Hurry, 95.

body asking for today? I started to develop a newfound love for walking, and as I mentioned earlier, yoga. I went on bike rides and started playing basketball, expanding my exercise options and discovering movement I found enjoyable.

The Sabbath creates margins my to-do lists never will. It's taught me while my life may be on hold for twenty-four hours, the rest of the world will continue to move and function just fine.

It's humbled me, shown me the gift of living a quiet life, and made me a less anxious presence.

Lifestyle of Recovery

I've found there are three phases to recovering from an eating disorder. The first is intervention. It's noticing you have a problem and taking the small and scary steps necessary to address the problem.

You can be hesitant in this phase and even in denial. You might quietly dip your toes in counseling, tell a friend or family member about your struggle, or go to a treatment facility.

The second phase is discovery. It's coming out of confusion and denial and gaining more understanding of your disorder, whether through information online, podcasts featuring other survivors, or books detailing things like the mind-body connection.

As a victim of an eating disorder starts to learn more of the "why," they are able to move forward by trying out some of the recovery steps they are learning about. This place can still be scary for some and usually consists of much trial and error.

Phase two is about finding what works for you. It's acknowledging your needs will be different than another person's needs, and it's being open to both the wins and losses you face.

Some might start a blog or Instagram in this phase to cultivate a safe space to share their journey.

Lastly is the third phase, which is lifestyle. In this phase, the victim starts to home in on their needs. They find two or three practices they can realistically implement into their lives long term to make recovery sustainable.

They might name their eating disorder and have a conversation with it when they feel tempted to restrict, binge, purge, or so on. They might have an accountability partner to reach out to when they're struggling, or they might resist diets of any kind and live a life of intuitive eating.

The biggest and most important thing in phase three is the person goes from being a victim to a survivor. They learn to view and accept their eating disorder as a part of them and can talk about it openly because they are no longer tied down by shame.

Overcoming perfection and hurry have been the two biggest things to have set me up for a lifestyle of recovery. Without the expectation of perfection, I can celebrate small wins and let go of limitations or times I've failed. I can keep moving forward without fear.

With a slower pace of life, the enemy has less of an opportunity to convince me I'm unworthy. There's more space for truth and for Jesus. He's making me new every day, sculpting me into the authentic version of myself I couldn't ever be on my own.

This quote says it perfectly:

> I have come to believe that we are destined to be opened by the living of our days, and whether we like it or not, whether we choose to participate or not, we will, in time, every one of us, wear the deeper part of who we are as a new skin.[72]

Similar to following Jesus, recovery must make it on your schedule, or it will never happen. It must become a part of your lifestyle.

So strap on your boots and get ready because the adventure awaiting you is one you don't want to miss. The adventure is calling you, now and forever.

---

72 Nepo, *The Book of Awakening*, 58.

CHAPTER 18

BELIEVING BEAUTIFUL

———

Slowly but surely, I'm learning who Carly is and what it means to live comfortably in Carly's skin. It used to feel like every day I was putting on a new mask and ignoring the fact none of them were truly me. Lately, my closet has become less crowded with masks and more filled by me. It feels good at times, but also scary, uncomfortable, and beautiful. So many of the things I once despised about myself have become qualities I'm proud to carry. I am happy to be me (most days). I'm starting to accept all of my good, and all of my bad.

My senior year of college was stressful, to say the least. I was enrolled in eighteen credits my last semester while working in between classes and leading a community of around fifteen people through my church.

I wasn't sure what was up next for me but knew I didn't want to spend another summer working in an office at an internship that was only supposed to last three months yet turned into a year.

After applying to graduate school and getting accepted, I realized it was just another thing I was doing because I thought I should. My scholarship foundation would help with the total cost, and because I felt out of options and knew I wanted to go back to school at some point, I thought it would give me more time to figure it all out.

But did I really want to devote two years to earn a master's degree I wasn't 100 percent sure was going to lead me to the future I wanted? No.

It didn't help I got back together with one of my ex-boyfriends who despised the idea of me staying in Portland to go to school because he wanted to move away from the city eventually.

Then one night, God brought to mind the idea of me living in Baker City for the summer. At first, I laughed at the thought because I couldn't imagine living with family after being on my own for the four years prior.

I'd also made a commitment to step into leadership in the church, and *what would people think if I were to walk away now? That's just not an option. My whole life is in Portland.*

I sat with the idea more and God, being the clever guy He is, started to reveal to me why He suggested it.

I was burnt out, my apartment was having multiple maintenance issues, and my family missed me. Earlier in the year, He opened me up to the idea of getting a roommate and I agreed, yet only if an opportunity arose with one of my close friends...which it never did.

If I move to Baker, I'll be living in my grandparents' guest house with my cousin on their property. Granted, she isn't exactly the kind of roommate I'm looking for, but maybe God wants to grow me in this season. Maybe I can learn from her, and she can learn from me.

I could take the summer off from work. I could finish my book. I could save money and help out with Grandpa. I'll get to spend more time with my mom, Marley, and Linkin. Maybe this is a good thing.

After having this spontaneous idea confirmed by leaders in the church, friends, family, and my boyfriend at the time, I decided to make the move.

Now, I'm going to be honest and say moving to eastern Oregon was one of the scariest things I've done. No, I wasn't moving to a foreign country where I didn't know anyone like when I traveled to Australia. Still, I was moving away from everything that had made up my life, weeks, and days, things I had really grown to rely on and love.

Parts of it were great, while other parts of it had me waking up anxious from all of the loss I was experiencing. I kept wondering, *Why on Earth did I move here? Who am I without school and work? Who am I without my friends and church?*

Eventually, I broke up with my boyfriend (this time for real) after remembering why it didn't work out in the past. I was drinking more than normal, making poor decisions, and trying to numb the pain. Having family nearby was exactly what I needed to prevent me from making other poor decisions or never having the heart to leave the relationship.

Soon, my cousin moved to Wyoming and I had the entire house to myself. I started to make some friends, friends from Portland were coming to visit me, I was going to visit them, and I was spending more time with my family than I ever had.

Cancer continued to invade parts of my grandpa's body, and my grandma couldn't do it all on her own. After taking him off chemo, we slowly watched his fragile body deteriorate day by day. But he never stopped fighting. He fought until the end, and he fought hard.

Being with my family, finding my rhythm, and seeing my papa's smile every day (even amidst the most grueling pain) gave me the energy to keep moving forward.

Little by little, I was reminded that in my rocky, unknown season, I still had a purpose. Although I had lost some things, I had gained some, too.

I got a job in the fall and started working at a physical therapy clinic where I taught a stretch class once a week and continued to learn the importance of taking care of my body.

I helped out Grandma and Grandpa every chance possible and got to relive certain memories I'd made with them after moving out of my dad's home in high school.

I was introduced to my now boyfriend who—similar to me—was only in eastern Oregon for a short time to be with his family. We started dating and have created a mountain of memories since.

Meanwhile, I was working with a story coach I happened to stumble upon at an unplanned trip to the farmer's market. He's who helped me nail down my writing process and finish this book.

What I've learned in the last year is most things in life can't be planned, and regardless of how well you map an idea out, it's likely you will be surprised by the curveballs thrown at you.

I've also learned that to accept a new path takes courage when you've got your teeth clenched tightly and your pride on the line.

But as you tell God, *That's not the plan*, you will slowly start to hear Him whisper back, *I've got something better*.

Trust that. Even in weak moments, trust Him.

Fear will try and rob you of joy, but remember our fear is the best guide we have, and joy can be found wherever you are.

Overcoming the Lack Mindset

In 2018, I changed my Instagram name from @carlyscounter to @believingbeautiful. I wanted my audience to not only take tasty recipes away from my page but also a true understanding that beauty can be found in all they do and in all they are. I wrote this book for similar reasons.

I want you, the reader, to Believe Beautiful for yourself, for others, and for this world.

You see, I spent so much of my life hiding under a rock because of my "lack" mindset.

There's not enough.
I'm not enough.
Nothing is ever enough.

From the minute I woke up, I'd start setting limits on myself about what I could or couldn't do when abundance was all around me. Abundance is all around *you*.

Chances are, you picked up this book because you suffer from a "lack" mindset too, which is why my ultimate goal is to remind you that you are not alone.

Exposing my raw journal entries and emotions is one of the most vulnerable things I've ever done. It terrified me. Yet, what terrified me even more was the thought of wearing a mask for the rest of my life, being the person I thought other people wanted me to be, and never discovering who the real Carly is.

I know what it's like to feel alone.
I know what it's like to feel shame.
I know what it's like to feel ugly.

When we vocalize these feelings, however, we start to realize they don't hold as much weight and power as we often give them. We start to realize we aren't as horrible and unloved as we once thought.

Vulnerability opens the door to healing and through healing we start to taste freedom.

My story is only one story. It is filled with *my* wounds, *my* doubts, *my* fears, and *my* struggles. I invited you along this journey in the beginning, and now it's your turn to invite someone along in your journey.

Tell your story confidently. Tell it bravely. People need to hear your voice because it matters.

Digging Deep

Ed Mylett once said, "You can't be yourself unless you love yourself, and you can't love yourself unless you believe in yourself."[73]

This hits deep for me.

It took me a long time to be myself because I didn't know how to love myself, and I couldn't love myself because I didn't know how to believe in myself.

---

73 Ed Mylett, "How Your Ego is Causing Failure!," May 6, 2020, in *The Ed Mylett Show*, produced by Ed Mylett, podcast, MP3 audio, 23:12.

Some days I still find myself in a lack mindset. I face days—sometimes weeks—where everything *just feels heavy.*

But my way of dealing with this heaviness is different than before because I rely less on my monsters to tell me lies I believe as truths, and I encourage myself.

I don't get on social media and post a selfie hoping I'll get a lot of likes and comments lifting me up and telling me how pretty I am.

Instead, I look in the mirror and I read the affirmations I listed at the end of chapter seven. I become my own cheerleader and say, *You can do it! I believe in you! Keep your head up. You are strong.*

In those moments, I remember my outward appearance isn't what makes me beautiful, and I give myself the attention I used to seek out from others.

Once I believe, I'm then able to love. Love being an action, not a feeling. I can look at my naked body in the mirror and compassionately accept and love what I see, even if I don't like what I see—the weight gain, the cellulite, the battle scars within.

The more I love myself, the more I start to become myself. Questioning and getting curious about the things that get in the way.

Why am I experiencing this negative feeling?
Why am I choosing to exercise?

Why am I wearing makeup?
Why do I believe I can't devote an entire day to rest?

If any of my answers to the above questions come out as lies, I finish the exercise by asking myself, *What is the truth?*

More than once, I've asked myself this question while entering the gym, and it's led me to exit seconds later because of faulty beliefs around why I should be exercising.

Another time, it inspired me to do a "no makeup challenge" for two weeks with a group of women.

I've taken breaks from social media, set boundaries with toxic people in my life, and prioritized the time, energy, and steps it takes to heal.

Through it all, I've tried to be transparent by sharing my highs and lows because this stuff is hard.

It's hard accepting the fact I am human, imperfect, and carry my own trauma.

Still, I am me. I love me, and I believe in me.

Four Simple Words

I'm still not sure where I will end up next. Will I write more books? Will I start a business? Will I go back to school? Get married? Start a family? It's all still up in the air and that's scary.

The difference between my fear before and my fear now is I know it's not my forever place. I'm confident, even on my worst days, *I'm right where I'm supposed to be.*

You are right where *you* are supposed to be.

I read through the book of Ephesians over and over after I moved east because I too need reminders I'm not defined by what I do.

As I've been saying goodbye to some of the untrue identity statements and belief systems I once carried, I've become more clear on who I am and how I want to cultivate meaning as I move through this life.

I want to thank you for accepting my invitation to learn with me through the chapters of this book. Although I may not know you personally, I have attained the utmost compassion in my heart for you, and it is my hope you leave this book with the certainty you are loved.

I pray you learn to accept the negative experiences in your life, recognizing the beauty they now have or will one day bring to your story.

Without darkness, there would be no light, and the contrast between the two is necessary.

There are four crucial things God put on my heart to share with the readers of this book, and to close, I'm going to share them with you.

The first is this: You are capable of the impossible and stronger than you think. It doesn't matter what the experiences of those around you have been, what has or hasn't been done. You are unique, meaning your story is unique, too.

So, whatever you're going through—no matter how big or small—you can and you will overcome it because the spirit of God dwells inside of you.[74]

Secondly: The narrow path is always more rewarding than the wide one. Friend, I'll be honest and say I'm still learning this. Over and over, I'm faced with the reality that what I think is going to lead to true life doesn't help me, and instead harms me. But there is beauty in coming to God and admitting you need His help in adversity, in relationships, and in an addiction.

The path to follow Him isn't easy, that's why it's narrow, and it's why you never have to travel it alone. Instead, you get to follow Jesus.

Third: Feelings will pass and truth will remain. I can't stress enough how important it is to acknowledge our feelings. In the same vein, it's important to distinguish feelings from reality. Meaning you can *feel* useless, but that doesn't mean you *are* useless. You can feel unworthy, yet we know from Ephesians and other passages in scripture you are beyond worthy and loved.

---

74   1 Cor. 3:16 (ESV).

Feelings do not equal identity. Of course, notice and explore your feelings, but don't go as far as to define yourself by them. God's truth will never run out, and any time you sense the enemy trying to convince you otherwise, revisit scripture and use it as your weapon in times of weakness. Our feelings have a tendency to lead us astray if we aren't careful, which is why revisiting a steady foundation you can trust in is key.

Finally, I want to leave you now with the four most important words in this book. From the very beginning, these words are what motivated me to keep writing. So, whether you are my friend or a stranger, near or far, a brother or sister, I want you to know deep in your bones and hear this:

You. Are. Good. Enough.

To end, I invite you to pray this over yourself, and if you can't, I will.

Father,
I come to You in faith, asking Your perfect love would comfort the ache of my soul. Would You erase any tension, worry, or fear I'm carrying, and would it just be me and You in this moment. I'm reminded without You I can do nothing.[75] Time and time again, I've tried and I've failed, and right now I need Your help. Would You renew my mind and help me to see myself how You see me? I pray the more I continue to look at the reflection of my life, the more I see the truth that I am fearfully and wonderfully made.[76] I believe in You, God, and

---

75   John 15:5 (ESV).
76   Ps. 139:14 (ESV).

ask Your goodness would navigate the unbelief I carry; to know and accept I'm worthy and—regardless of my past, present, and future—I am good enough. You don't weigh me on a scale next to anyone else. You are forgiving and merciful. Teach me how to be more like You, in my failure, radiate grace, to show strength in weakness. Fill me with Your love and compassion, so I might share that same kind of love and compassion with myself and others. I thank You for every bump in the road You make beautiful and trust You will continue to pour down blessings on the path of my life. Amen.

RESOURCES

Organizations:

- Families Empowered And Supporting Treatment for Eating Disorders (F.E.A.S.T.)

- National Association of Anorexia Nervosa and Associated Disorders (ANAD)
  Helpline: (630) 577-1330

- National Eating Disorders Association (NEDA)
  Helpline: (800) 931-2237

- The Butterfly Foundation
  Helpline: 1800 ED HOPE

Books:

- *Eating in the Light of the Moon: How Women Can Transform Their Relationship with Food Through Myths, Metaphors, and Storytelling* by Anita Johnston

- *Gaining a Life: The Untold Story of My Eating Disorder & Recovery by Emily* Formea

- *Hunger* by Roxane Gay

- *Intuitive Eating: A Revolutionary Program That Works* by Evelyn Tribole and Elyse Resch

- *Lighter Than My Shadow* by Katie Green

Films & Documentaries:

- *I Am Maris: Portrait of a Young Yogi*

- *Miss Americana*

- *To the Bone*

Podcasts:

- *Let's Thrive* with Emily Feikls

- *The Recovery Warrior Show* with Jessica Flint

- *Well and Weird* with Holly Lowery

YouTube Channels:

- Mallory Page

- Natacha Océane

- *What Mia Did Next*

Instagram Accounts:

- @dietculturesucks

- @dietfree.nutritionist

- @dietitiandeanna

- @eatwithcare

- @itselizadordelman

- @juliealedbetter

- @kellyu

- @mikzazon

- @p.bodii

- @triadwarriors

ACKNOWLEDGMENTS

To see what started out as a random thought in my journal evolve into a complete book full of vulnerabilities and important messages is a humbling experience I wouldn't trade for anything. The journey has been extensive, but the support I've received has been massive. Similar to recovering from my eating disorder, I could have never done this alone. Through my process of writing *Good Enough*, I've learned the best things in life only get better with a loving community by your side. My community made the long nights bearable and brought the early mornings within reach by helping me breakthrough every difficulty so I could rise up stronger than before.

Thank you first and foremost to my family, Mom, Dad, and Kyle, for letting me share parts of your story to tell my own.

Thank you, Stephen Howard, for helping me discover my writing process. I'll never forget showing up to one of our coaching sessions with the themes of my book and connections I'd made drawn on the back of a broken-down cereal box.

Thank you, Ronnie Still, for comforting and encouraging me through the writer's block, tough emotions, and stress. From the day I first told you about my dream to finish *Good Enough*, to the time we stayed up until midnight recording the video footage for my pre-launch campaign, you were there for it all, and you never stopped believing in me.

Thank you New Degree Press for playing the biggest role in the creation and publication of *Good Enough*. You made the steps to publish my first book seamless and within reach. Emily Price, thank you especially for being available to answer my millions of questions, and for strengthening my manuscript through your advice and wisdom. You have been a friend to me from start to finish, and I'm beyond grateful to know you.

Lastly, a *huge* thank you to everyone who pre-ordered the eBook, paperback, or multiple copies of *Good Enough*. Thank you also to those who donated to my pre-launch campaign or helped spread the word and build momentum around *Good Enough*. You all helped me publish a book I am proud of, and I couldn't have done it without you:

Jennifer Newberg*	Tiffany Rhodes
Janet McLean	Alexandra Crouse
Robert & Joan Wimmer*	Susan Zellweger
Ellen Neltner	Justin McKinney
Laura Harshbarger	Craig Mclean
Rozalyn Goldberg	Jeanice Myrtue
Melissa Powers	Abby Winstead
Sandra & Ed Neustel	Rebecca A Carter
Moriah Gingerich	Sheryl Blankenship

Kathy Jacobson
Denise Cummins
Tyson & Lexy Froemke
Katie Koniakowsky
Emily Formea
Danielle Wagner
Stefanie Mathers
Pamela Hoene
Martina Duggan
Courtnie Taylor
Megan Hall
Alisa Sheets*
Anna Edington
Eric Koester
Maureen Joseph
Reanne Mae Macalintal
Diane Amelia Read
Kristina Bullock
Kyle Newberg &
Ama Jackson*
Meredith Work
Emma James
Jason Morris
JoEllen & Ron Still*
Natalie King
Karen L Newberg*
Bella Gotts*
Lea Gettle
Garrett V Robison
Robin Dorsey Cosley
Tanner C Dorsey
Crystal Kimball

Chrissy Shanks*
Emma Andrews
Martha Kellams
Lorna Anderson
Tanya Griffiths
Jessica Vanasse
Katie Toomb
Erin Martineau
Leah Hayes
Leslie Carroll
Susan & Mike Morch
Kyle Gamez
Jenna Morch
Tami DuFault-Toomb
Annie Calhoun
Lisa Highsmith-Miller
Jody & Pete Sipos*
Kerri Bain
Kim Zinn
Beth Moore
Ashley da Silva
Anthea Stephens
Tami Ainsworth
Barbara Snow
Wendi Kamlade
Nancy May
Makenna Wimmer
Gitanjali Sterling
Ellen Reece
Sarah Dale
Morgan Wimmer*
Kenzie Kilborn

Scott & Kelly Frost*
Susan Ford
Lori Patterson*
Todd Newberg & Emily
Wuthenow Leland*
Claire Wheeler
Cayla Pruett
Scott Stclair
Michele Burd
Daisy Garber
Margaux Fougere
Angelina Ota
Haylee Hafner
Beverly M Smith
Becca Salmonson
Andy Borbon
Elaina Bauer
Monica Maurer
Key Dickey*
Shayne Reagan
Lynne Ewing
Shilpa Sarah
Sarah Tribett
Mary Armijo*
Peter Becker
T Bourgeois
Tanya Maxwell
Anita Choi*
Erin Wood
Angie Reams
Jessica Grose
Ashley Silverii

Aleksandra Rosca
Sara Melton
Roslyn Smith
Nicole Spindler
Mary Stevenson
Alicia Webb
Emily Monroe
Misty Ortiz
Doug Phillips*
Kate Johnston
Jena Long
Don Knight*
Steven Ostling
Jason Stone*
Alicia Larson
Aika Griffith*
KaryAnn Lane
Kyle Millar
Samantha Solomon
DyAnn McVicker
Mia de Haan
Hannah Alley
Andrea Weimer
Amanda Vorderstrasse
Victoria Frelich
Jenae Brinster
Adrienne Hill-Strathy
Daniel Mills
Danielle Herr
Patricia Still
Ronald Barrett
Bri Grunow

Edgar C Mayen
Macey Frei
Marcus Spires
Chad Nissen*
Madison Kelly
Colleen Shank
Jenifer Caudle
Mary Mahoney
Rachel Thompson
Sierra Giddings
Deanna Chambers Varner
Kavic Belcastro
Lori Romeo
Tanya Hug
Amanda Pierce
Stephanie Chisum
Amber Kellett
Nicolette Wise
Danielle Koski
Hannah Steuck

Mohammed Almarzouq
Shantel Durski
Laura Saxe-O'Brien
Anne Nemec
Candice Escobar
Julianne Robinson
Jacqueline Spradlin
Erika Lemerande
Katherine Palmer
Chelsea Azarcon
Kari King
Cassie Morrissey
Zoya Altuhova
Kaci Cheeseman
Michelle Roeger
Halie Sadowsky
Jonie Froemke
Aranza Lechuga
Castiney Stallard
Latia Vadbunker

* = Multiple copies/campaign contributions.

APPENDIX

Introduction

Brewerton, Timothy D. "Eating Disorders, Trauma, and Comorbidity: Focus on PTSD." *Eating Disorders: The Journal of Treatment & Prevention* 15, no. 4 (2007): 285-304. https://doi.org/10.1080/10640260701454311.

Chesney, Edward, Guy M. Goodwin, and Seena Fazel. "Risks of All-Cause and Suicide Mortality in Mental Disorders: A Meta-Review." *World Psychiatry* 13 no. 2 (2014): 153-160. https://doi.org/10.1002/wps.20128.

Hudson, James I., Eva Hiripi, Harrison G. Pope, and Ronald C. Kessler. "The Prevalence and Correlates of Eating Disorders in the National Comorbidity Survey Replication." *Biological Psychiatry* 61, no. 3 (2007): 348–358. https://doi.org/10.1016/j.biopsych.2006.03.040.

Le Grange, Daniel, Sonja A. Swanson, Scott J. Crow, and Kathleen R. Merikangas. "Eating Disorder Not Otherwise Specified Presentation in the Us Population." *International*

Journal of Eating Disorders 45, no. 5 (2012): 711-718. https://doi.org/10.1002/eat.22006.

Chapter 1

National Eating Disorders Association. "Eating Disorder Myths." Accessed September 3, 2020. https://www.nationaleatingdisorders.org/toolkit/parent-toolkit/eating-disorder-myths.

Nepo, Mark. *The Book of Awakening: Having the Life You Want by Being Present to the Life You Have.* Newburyport: Conari Press, 2000.

Riso, Don Richard, and Russ Hudson. *Personality Types: Using the Enneagram for Self-Discovery.* Boston: Houghton Mifflin, 1987.

Trauma-Informed Care Implementation Resource Center. "What Is Trauma?" Accessed August 22, 2020. https://www.traumainformedcare.chcs.org/what-is-trauma/.

Chapter 2

Riso, Don Richard, and Russ Hudson. *Personality Types: Using the Enneagram for Self-Discovery.* Boston: Houghton Mifflin, 1987.

Chapter 3

Dawson, Christian. "You Wouldn't Understand." August 23, 2020. In *Bridgetown Audio Podcast.* Produced by

Bridgetown Church. Podcast, MP3 audio, 44:00. https://
podcasts.apple.com/us/podcast/bridgetown-audio-podcast/
id84246334?i=1000488967107.

Hollis, Rachel. *Girl, Wash Your Face*. Nashville: Thomas
Nelson, 2018.

Silk, Danny. *Culture of Honor: Sustaining a Supernatural
Environment*. Shippensburg: Destiny Image Publishers, 2009.

Walden University. "MSN Course Insight: The Three 'E's' of
Trauma Every Nurse Practitioner Should Know." Accessed
September 3, 2020. https://www.waldenu.edu/online-mas-
ters-programs/master-of-science-in-nursing/resource/
msn-course-insight-the-three-e-s-of-trauma-every-nurse-
practitioner-should-know.

Wheeler, Claire Michaels. *10 Simple Solutions to Stress: How
to Tame Tension & Start Enjoying Life*. Oakland: New Harbinger Publication, 2007.

Chapter 4

Chapter 5

Brown, Brené. *The Gifts of Imperfection: Let Go of Who You
Think You're Supposed to Be and Embrace Who You Are*. Center City: Hazelden Publishing, 2010.

Lewis, C. S. *The Four Loves: An Exploration of the Nature of
Love*. Boston: Mariner Books Houghton Mifflin Harcourt,
1960.

Chapter 6

Riso, Don Richard, and Russ Hudson. *Personality Types: Using the Enneagram for Self-Discovery*. Boston: Houghton Mifflin, 1987.

Chapter 7

DeSanctis, Emily. "What Emotional Abuse Really Means." One Love Foundation. Accessed August 30, 2020. https://www.joinonelove.org/learn/emotional-abuse-really-means/.

Patu, Shantel. "Can Words Really Hurt Me?" *The Gottman Institute: A Research-Based Approach to Relationships*, May 29, 2019. https://www.gottman.com/blog/can-words-really-hurt-me/.

Chapter 8

Brown, Brené. *The Gifts of Imperfection: Let Go of Who You Think You're Supposed to Be and Embrace Who You Are*. Center City: Hazelden Publishing, 2010.

Chapter 9

Morin, Amy. *13 Things Mentally Strong Women Don't Do: Own Your Power, Channel Your Confidence, and Find Your Authentic Voice for a Life of Meaning and Joy*. New York: William Morrow, 2018.

Chapter 10

Case, Sarajane. "Enneagram and Relationships." July 2, 2020. In *Enneagram & Coffee*. Produced by Sarajane Case. Podcast, MP3 audio, 45:00. https://podcasts.apple.com/us/podcast/enneagram-and-relationships/id1447982978?i=1000481764233.

Johnston, Anita. *Eating in the Light of the Moon: How Women Can Transform Their Relationships with Food through Metaphors & Storytelling*. Carlsbad: Gurze, 1996.

Mayo Clinic. "Body Dysmorphic Disorder." Accessed October 6, 2020. https://www.mayoclinic.org/diseases-conditions/body-dysmorphic-disorder/symptoms-causes/syc-20353938.

Nepo, Mark. *The Book of Awakening: Having the Life You Want by Being Present to the Life You Have*. Newburyport: Conari Press, 2000.

Chapter 11

Morgan, Ian Cron, and Suzanne Stabile. *The Road Back to You: An Enneagram Journey to Self-Discovery*. Westmont: InterVarsity Press, 2016.

Nepo, Mark. *The Book of Awakening: Having the Life You Want by Being Present to the Life You Have. Newburyport*: Conari Press, 2000.

Chapter 12

Christ, Erin. "Weight Gain and the 'Thin' Ideal + Overcoming Diet Culture with Erin Christ." August 19, 2020. In *Let's Thrive*. Produced by Emily Feikls. Podcast, MP3 audio, 53:00. https://podcasts.apple.com/us/podcast/lets-thrive/id1450703792?i=1000488550837.

Culbert, Kristen N., Sarah E. Racine, and Kelly L. Klump. "Research Review: What We Have Learned about the Causes of Eating Disorders - A Synthesis of Sociocultural, Psychological, and Biological Research." *The Journal of Child Psychology and Psychiatry* 56, no. 11 (June 2015): 1141-1164. https://doi.org/10.1111/jcpp.12441.

Johnston, Anita. *Eating in the Light of the Moon: How Women Can Transform Their Relationships with Food through Metaphors & Storytelling*. Carlsbad: Gurze, 1996.

Riso, Don Richard, and Russ Hudson. *Personality Types: Using the Enneagram for Self-Discovery*. Boston: Houghton Mifflin, 1987.

Chapter 13

Brown, Brené. *The Gifts of Imperfection: Let Go of Who You Think You're Supposed to Be and Embrace Who You Are*. Center City: Hazelden Publishing, 2010.

Morin, Amy. *13 Things Mentally Strong Women Don't Do: Own Your Power, Channel Your Confidence, and Find Your*

Authentic Voice for a Life of Meaning and Joy. New York: William Morrow, 2018.

Chapter 14

Chastain, Ragen. "Recognizing and Resisting Diet Culture." *National Eating Disorder Association* (blog). September 13, 2020. https://www.nationaleatingdisorders.org/blog/recognizing-and-resisting-diet-culture.

Chapter 15

Alderton, Dolly. *Everything I Know About Love: A Memoir.* New York: HarperCollins, 2020.

Chapter 16

Brown, Brené. *Daring Greatly: How the Courage to Be Vulnerable Transforms the Way We Live, Love, Parent, and Lead.* New York: Avery Publishing, 2012.

Morgan, Ian Cron and Suzanne Stabile. *The Road Back to You: An Enneagram Journey to Self-Discovery.* Westmont: InterVarsity Press, 2016.

Morin, Amy. *13 Things Mentally Strong Women Don't Do: Own Your Power, Channel Your Confidence, and Find Your Authentic Voice for a Life of Meaning and Joy.* New York: William Morrow, 2018.

Chapter 17

Comer, John Mark. *The Ruthless Elimination of Hurry: How to Stay Emotionally Healthy and Spiritually Alive in the Chaos of the Modern World*. London: Hodder & Stoughton, 2019.

Hollis, Rachel. *Girl, Wash Your Face*. Nashville: Thomas Nelson, 2018.

Nepo, Mark. *The Book of Awakening: Having the Life You Want by Being Present to the Life You Have*. Newburyport: Conari Press, 2000.

Chapter 18

Mylett, Ed. "How Your Ego is Causing Failure!" May 6, 2020. In *The Ed Mylett Show*. Produced by Ed Mylett. Podcast, MP3 audio, 23:12. https://podcasts.apple.com/us/podcast/how-your-ego-is-causing-failure/id1181233130?i=1000437308309?i=1000437308309.